WHY DOES NO ONE IN MY BOOKS LOOK LIKE ME?

The Center for the Study of the New South in The University of North Carolina at Charlotte's College of Liberal Arts & Sciences promotes discourse and dialogue on a rich and diverse constellation of topics and ideas relating to the New South. Known as the period of regional history from the end of the Civil War to the modern era, the New South offers a bold tapestry of history, culture, social movements, and political issues ripe for reflection and study. The Center's programming theme for 2017 was "Growing Up Southern" and supported by a UNC Charlotte Chancellor's Diversity Challenge Grant.

# WHY DOES NO ONE IN MY BOOKS LOOK LIKE ME?

*Tobe* and Ongoing Questions about Race, Representation, and Identity

EDITED BY

Ashli Quesinberry Stokes

*An Essay Collection Compiled from the Center for the Study of the New South and Charlotte Teachers Institute First Annual Book Club Experience*

UNC CHARLOTTE | CENTER FOR THE STUDY OF THE NEW SOUTH

Suggested citation: Ashli Quesinberry Stokes, ed. Why Does No One In
My Books Look Like Me?: Tobe and Ongoing Questions about Race,
Representation, and Identity. Charlotte: Center for the Study of the New
South, UNC Charlotte, 2018.
doi: https://doi.org/10.5149/9781469642505_Stokes

Library of Congress Cataloging-in-Publication Data
ISBN 978-1-4696-4168-3 (paperback)
ISBN 978-1-4696-4250-5 (ebook)

Billingsville Leadership Academy and Grier Heights Community Center
6:00–8:30 p.m.

Participants discussing *Tobe* at the Tobe Book Club Experience, April 26, 2017.

*Tobe*, published in 1939 by the UNC Press, was one of the first-ever children's books depicting African American life in rural North Carolina. It was written by a white woman in response to a black child's wondering why he didn't see children like himself in books. The book club experience discussion explored *Tobe* as a springboard for discussions about race, racial representation, and identity.

The event was sponsored by PricewaterhouseCoopers and UNC Charlotte's Chancellor's Diversity Fund, in partnership with the Center for the Study of the New South and Charlotte Teachers Institute (CTI).

The Center for the Study of the New South in UNC Charlotte's College of Liberal Arts & Sciences promotes discourse and dialogue on a rich and diverse constellation of topics and ideas relating to the New South. The Center's theme for 2017 was "Growing Up Southern."

CTI is an educational partnership among Charlotte-Mecklenburg Schools, UNC Charlotte, and Johnson C. Smith University. Since 2009, CTI has served more than four hundred fifty teachers who have written more than seven hundred original curriculum units for more than 103,000 CMS students.

## ACKNOWLEDGMENTS

There are many people who helped make this project a reality, and we would like to take a moment to thank them here.

To Dr. Benjamin Filene, thank you for sharing the initial list of discussion questions, for offering introductions to the text at our event and in this volume, and for your deep insight into this remarkable story.

To Dr. Nancy Gutierrez, Dean, College of Liberal Arts and Sciences at UNC Charlotte, for supporting the Center for the Study of the New South and the Charlotte Teachers Institute, as well as for participating in the Tobe experience and introducing what we hope will become a regular publication series.

To all of our essayists and participants: thank you for taking the time to share your reflections with our Charlotte community.

To Lynn Roberson, for taking amazing pictures to preserve and represent the Book Club Experience.

To Robin Mara and Kayla Modlin, thank you for your help in keeping us organized, on track, and in the black.

To the UNC Press and its Office of Scholarly Publishing Services, thank you for support of this unique project by way of the Thomas W. Ross Fund Publishing Grant and for providing an outlet for this type of work.

To PricewaterhouseCoopers and UNC Charlotte's Chancellor's Diversity Fund, thank you for your financial support of this project.

And to Clay McCauley Jr.: thank you for asking the question.

Participant copy of *Tobe* at the reception.

# CONTENTS

# Introduction to the *Tobe* Book Club Experience

DR. NANCY A. GUTIERREZ | DEAN, COLLEGE OF LIBERAL ARTS AND SCIENCES, UNC CHARLOTTE

I was privileged to participate in the community conversation about *Tobe*, hosted by UNC Charlotte's Center for the Study of the New South and the Charlotte Teachers Institute. For more than an hour, on the evening of April 26, 2017, I talked about this children's book with a math teacher, an English teacher, a college instructor, and a UNC Press editor. We were women and men, white and black, American, and Jamaican.

In the introduction to this volume, Dr. Benjamin Filene lays open the challenges in pinning down the nature of the book. As a literary scholar myself, I know that the volume's very contradictions are its meaning. The genesis of the writing, the invention of the story with its "actor" characters, its reception by readers in the 1940s and 1950s, and its muddled after-story all are part of the book's cultural and political moment and textual significance.

However, as fascinating a cultural product as *Tobe* is, on that evening, its import was almost secondary, as it served as the occasion for community members to share their own stories—and the stories were wide-ranging. Not only did my new-found friends and I, all educators in one way or another, talk about our specific classrooms and individual students, about what this book might mean in their lives, but we also discussed our own coming of age and our own experiences in different parts of the country (or world), as we learned about race and power.

Who tells the story, as we know, is the person (or the people) who gets to make sense of the world. My friends and I told our stories—yes, occasioned by this book full of ambiguities and inconsistencies—and our stories have now become a small part of who we are. And now, the transitory occasion of reading and talking about *Tobe* on a beautiful evening in April has been transformed into this collection of essays. I invite you to continue reading, to participate in the storytelling about *Tobe* that started last spring, and to make your own sense of the world.

# *Tobe*

The Center for the Study of the New South,
Charlotte Teachers Institute, and a Remarkable Event

SCOTT GARTLAN AND ASHLI STOKES | UNC CHARLOTTE

In Charlotte, we wanted something big. Something to hold our attention and challenge our assumptions. Something culturally relevant at a time when so much of the city's collective identity was in flux. Something to orient our current feelings about a time and place in a larger context. So, surprisingly, we turned to a children's book written in the 1930s.

"Why does no one in books look like me?" is the title of this collection of essays written about a book discussion of the children's book, *Tobe*, written by Stella Gentry Sharpe in 1939 and published by the UNC Press. This question also motivated our interest in moving forward with this project that we hoped would lead to a meaningful, interactive community conversation about race and identity. Looking into *Tobe* after learning about it from a colleague at the Levine Museum of the New South, we consulted with experts in the field of children's literature who shared that this book represents a historically significant contribution to the field. It is recognized as one of the first-ever children's books depicting African American life in rural North Carolina. We became fascinated with this central question, not only because of the historical weight of an African American boy who asked this question eighty years ago, but also because of the relevance for our lives today. *Tobe* is about a six-year-old boy who grew up on a farm in North Carolina. It tells the story of his experiences growing up with his family, written in a way that is straightforward and accessible for all readers. The original book is filled with beautiful black-and-white photographs taken by Charles Farrell. They represent the main character, Clay Junior, nicknamed Tobe by the author, and his brothers and sisters, mother and father, and animals on his farm. The juxtaposition of the simple sentences and striking photographs come together in a stunning way to document the experiences of growing up in the South during the 1930s.

In researching *Tobe's* motivating question, we discovered a study that examined the prevalence of minority main characters in children's literature. The Cooperative Children's Book Center at the University of Wisconsin–Madison reviewed 3,200 children's books published in the United States in 2015 and found that only 14 percent had black, Latino, Asian, or Native American main characters. We then realized that it is entirely possible that the great-grandchildren of Clay Junior's could still be wondering why their books did not have characters that looked like them. It was from this beginning that we set forth to convene a group of Charlotteans—educators, parents, students, business leaders, and community activists—to gather for an evening in the spring of 2017 to discuss *Tobe*.

This project was the culmination of many great people's efforts over the course of nine months focused on a singular purpose: to gather Charlotteans for a discussion about *Tobe*. Although our efforts resulted in the collection of essays you have in this book, it started with very humble beginnings. The first conversation we had in August 2016 at the university coffee shop led to our guiding focus for this project: book club-style discussion that represented the diverse Charlotte community we valued. We looked at diversity broadly— racial, economic, age, gender, occupational, educational, and geographical. We knew that if we worked hard to bring together a truly diverse group of people we would come close to representing the many voices in our Charlotte community.

One of our first challenges was to identify a venue that connected with *Tobe*. With the help of local historians, we located Billingsville Leadership Academy and the Grier Heights Community Center as the perfect locations mixing history, community, and school in a nod to experiences depicted in *Tobe*. Billingsville is a K–5 school in the Charlotte-Mecklenburg School system with a rich history and tradition. Adjacent to the current school is the original building for the Billingsville Rosenwald School built in 1927 and listed on the National Register of Historic Places. This school was part of the eight hundred such schools in North Carolina created through a partnership between Jewish American businessman Julius Rosenwald and African American leader Booker T. Washington to serve African American children. Recently, the original school building was renovated and reopened as the Grier Heights Community Center, becoming a hub in the Grier Heights neighborhood, one

Billingsville Rosenwald School at Grier Heights Community Center, built in 1927.

of Charlotte's oldest African American neighborhoods. Under the leadership of longtime resident and graduate of Billingsville School, Gloria Green, we found a great way to showcase the center's place in Charlotte history.

In the end, the event was called the "*Tobe* Community Book Club Experience." Green hosted a reception at Grier Heights Community Center for the seventy guests. A local caterer provided good southern food as people sat at tables eating and sharing stories about their jobs, families, and expectations for the book discussion. We then exited the center, walked through Billingsville's courtyard complete with beautiful gardens, and into the school's gym where round tables were set up for the discussion. A total of nine tables were spread out on the gym floor, each with a table number and list of participants. We assigned seats ahead of time to encourage guests to meet new people through conversation. The evening started with a brief welcome from us, then a presentation from Benjamin Filene, professor of history and director of public history at UNC Greensboro. Filene studied *Tobe* extensively and interviewed the real-life people who were featured in the book. He shared that, although the book might read as a memoir of sorts of this boy's life, it is in fact closer to a work of fiction. The original boy who observed that characters in books didn't look like him, in fact, wasn't the boy photographed in the final book, raising

Participants walking through the gardens from the historic Billingsville Rosenwald School to the current Billingsville Elementary School.

the question of authenticity and who gets to tell whose story. That question was also of great interest to our participants and is reflected in their essays in this volume.

The nine table discussions took the better part of an hour. With Filene's help, we shared discussion questions that explored issues "between the pages" about words and images in the book, and issues "beyond the pages" about broader questions related to our lives and times. After the table discussions, we asked one member of each table to share some highlights. Each person identified the significance and relevance of *Tobe*, but not always in the same way. Some found the book to represent positive images of African American life during a time when there might not have been many such depictions, particularly in books accessible in rural North Carolina. Others found the author's status as a white female to be problematic, lacking the cultural experience to tell the story of an African American boy and his family. These are a couple of the themes that are explored in the essays that make up this collection.

This collection of essays represents a critical look into how contemporary Charlotteans understand *Tobe*'s place in history and its relevance for our current times. The essayists tackle a variety of themes that emerged from our discussions: an English professor unpacks authorship and authenticity; a school district coordinator explores identity and race; a community leader examines the book's particular time and place; a political science undergraduate student wonders about its relevance today; a nonprofit director reflects on photography's role in telling the story; a Spanish language professor appreciates the organic nature of the discourse; an Africana studies professor questions the ultimate meaning of *Tobe*; a historically black university professor compares *Tobe* to *Dick and Jane*; an elementary school media teacher explores race and culture in picture books; and finally, a school principal highlights the importance of telling one's own story.

We hope your experience in reading these essays gives you a sense of being there at our event in April 2017 at the Grier Heights Community Center and the Billingsville Leadership Academy. More important, however, we hope that you take forward a deeper appreciation for Stella Gentry Sharpe's book, *Tobe*, and use it as a springboard for conversations in your homes and communities about the times in which we live and how difference is a unifying theme we all share.

# Introducing *Tobe* to New Audiences

BENJAMIN FILENE, PH.D. | UNC GREENSBORO

T*obe* is hopelessly dated; *Tobe* speaks to our times.
*Tobe* is progressive; *Tobe* is retrograde.
*Tobe* is fiction; *Tobe* is documentary.

*Tobe* is not great literature. Well, okay but. . . . can it provoke great discussion?

The Center for the Study of the New South (CSNS) and Charlotte Teachers Institute (CTI)'s community conversation in spring 2017 aimed to probe these tensions and to resist easy answers. Seventy teachers, students, community leaders, and citizens from across the city had read Stella Sharpe's 1939 children's book *Tobe* and came together to reflect. I had been working for many years on a public history project about *Tobe*, so organizers Scott Gartlan and Ashli Stokes asked me to set the stage for the conversations with a ten-minute introduction. I shared some basic background on the book and my research, but our strategy was mostly to allow participants to come at the book fresh—*not* to answer all the questions a reader would have. We wanted to leave room for what reading as an experience is all about: honest encounters between one's inner thoughts and a world beyond us, between oneself and one's neighbors, between past and present.

In our small-group discussions, we grappled with the tensions embedded in the book: its troubling datedness and troubling timeliness; its progressiveness and its limits; its hokeyness and its humanity. By not trying to pin *Tobe* down, we allowed it to open up and reveal the power of a book—and this book—to speak to enduring questions about how we see ourselves and one another. As the rich personal accounts in this volume show, as we talked through *Tobe* at our tables, the book began to resonate in ways new and unexpected. And, for the moment at least, it helped us to draw new lines of connection.

That very open-endedness resonates with what drew me to *Tobe* in the first place and led me to imagine it as the center of a multifaceted project—one that eventually involved oral histories, museum exhibitions, and a new edition of the book.[1] I stumbled across *Tobe* in the archives of the North Carolina Collection at the University of North Carolina in Chapel Hill, and immediately I was struck by the photographs. Who were these people? What were they thinking on the day these photos were taken? What did they think of the resulting images (did they even see them)? How did this moment and this book come about?

The dust jacket from the 1939 book offers the first story behind the story. It recounts that in the mid-1930s, an African American boy asked his neighbor, a white schoolteacher, a simple question: "Why does no one in my books look like me?" She began to wonder the same thing and set out to write a different kind of children's book: one that featured African American characters in a way that countered the grossly stereotyped depictions of most children's literature of the time. This would be a dignified, true-to-life story of her young neighbor and his family. It would be Tobe's story.

Except the boy who asked the question was not named Tobe. He was Clay McCauley Jr. He lived in rural Orange County, North Carolina. At the time, his father was a tenant farmer, renting land that belonged to Luther Sharpe. Sharpe's wife, Stella, was a schoolteacher in nearby Hillsborough.[2] No one knows why Stella gave Clay the nickname Tobe in the book she wrote about him and his family. But the other names in the book—Raeford, twins Alvis and Alton, William and Rufus—match those of Clay's siblings. And their life on the farm matches the life of work and play that the young McCauleys lived.

Except that the photographs weren't taken on the McCauley farm and those

---

1. I recorded two dozen oral histories, which are archived at UNC Chapel Hill's Southern Oral History Program: https://sohp.org/oral-history-interviews/. My exhibition, *Where Is Tobe? Unfolding Stories of Childhood, Race, and Rural Life in North Carolina*, opened at the North Carolina Collection Gallery at UNC from October 2014 through March 2015. A new version of the exhibition, *Reading, Writing, Race: One Children's Book and the Power of Stories* is scheduled to travel to North Carolina sites beginning in spring 2018. The UNC Press is publishing a new, critical edition of *Tobe*, for which I am writing accompanying essays (forthcoming 2019).

2. The town spelled its name "Hillsboro" from the nineteenth century until 1965; see Erin Weeks, "Hillsborough, Hillsboro Change a Conundrum," *News of Orange County* (September 26, 2014): http://www.newsoforange.com/news/article_586a7f2c-44d0-11e4-820a-2fabe10d35b4.html.

aren't McCauleys in the pictures. Letters in the archives at UNC show that Sharpe did take photos of the McCauley children to illustrate her book; but the story goes that the quality of the images wasn't high enough for a printed book, and by the time the UNC Press was ready to go forward with the project, the children were too old, and they could no longer play the roles of themselves.

So the UNC Press hired a professional photographer, Charles Farrell, and told him to "find Tobe." Farrell had taken hundreds of photographs for the Greensboro *Daily News* and ran a local art shop. For this assignment, he went to an African American neighborhood right down the road, an area called Goshen. He may have known of it because a woman who worked as a domestic in his home went to church there. In any case, Farrell drove up to rural Goshen, just outside the city limits and, the story goes, he met a boy. That boy was Charles Winslow Garner. Friends knew him as "Windy." Farrell had found his "Tobe." Over the next several months, Farrell took photos of Windy, his parents, siblings, cousins, and friends: the Garners, Herbins, and Goinses. The photographs richly documented the children's day-to-day lives—their actual homes, school, and church; and at the same time, the photos staged scenes that enabled them to stand in for characters in a fictionalized story.

A children's book might seem an unlikely match for a scholarly publisher like the UNC Press, but the time was right for *Tobe*. In the 1920s and 1930s, the press had published a series of cutting-edge books on African American culture and the sociology, economics, and culture of race. Also, the crisis of the Great Depression had caused a surge of interest in documenting the power and dignity of the "common man and woman"—from Dust Bowl migrants in poignant *Life* magazine photos to post office murals across the country featuring heroic farmers to a folk music revival in Washington and New York.

Others had pushed to reform the world of children's literature before. W. E. B. DuBois published a magazine in 1920, *The Brownie's Book*, that told affirming stories about children of color. In 1938, Ellis Credle, a white author, published *The Flop-Eared Hound*, another book illustrated with photographs that featured rural black characters who did not speak in dialect.

So *Tobe* was not the first or only children's book to positively depict African American children; but the book was taken seriously by progressive educators and advocates, receiving positive reviews in newspapers and magazines across the country. By 1945, the book had sold twenty-one thousand copies. There was talk of a sequel, and Sharpe wrote the text for one, *Tobe's Cousins*, for which Farrell took photos, but it went nowhere. Sharpe went on to teach in Hillsbor-

Example of *Tobe's*
photography style.

ough for another quarter century. Farrell increasingly suffered from mental illness; in the 1940s, he had a lobotomy and never worked again.

Tellingly, *Tobe* was not the last effort to open children's literature to characters of color. The need to remake the world of children's books met with another surge of interest a generation later in the 1960s. And the issue is gaining traction again today, as educators, activists, parents, and readers recognize the power of seeing oneself in literature. Every generation, it seems, has to fight this battle anew. So the tide did not simply turn with *Tobe*, but the book did help advance a conversation that was at the cutting edge in its time and remains so in ours.

In this discussion of reactions and repercussions, what about the people at the center of *Tobe*'s story, the ones named and depicted on the pages themselves? The answers are even more complicated than I had expected. Shortly after the book's publication, the archives show, Arthur Garner, father of the boy photographed as Tobe, threatened a lawsuit because his family had not been paid for appearing in the book. Furious, photographer Charles Farrell pushed back. The dispute appears to have been settled, although the archives do not reveal how it was resolved.

Mostly, the people depicted in the book didn't hear of it again for decades, in some cases until seventy years after its publication, when I called them and asked to talk to them about it. In the oral interviews I recorded, Goshen residents who had been children when *Tobe* was published recall feeling proud to see it in their library. Some who went on to become teachers recall that they taught the book in their classrooms. Charles Garner, photographed as Tobe, came back to Goshen for the seventy-fifth anniversary of the book's publication and shared his recollections with the church's congregation, where he was embraced as a favorite son and returning celebrity.

Indeed, most of the current and former Goshen residents with whom I spoke see the book as a point of pride. To them, *Tobe* is an affirming story, one that documents a place and a way of life that they fear could be forgotten. This reaction makes sense when one considers how painfully few traces of Goshen appear in the official historical record (I've looked). *Tobe* becomes, to Goshen residents and their descendants, a memory book.

These interviews taught me that a children's story that I blithely labeled as fiction has an ongoing real-life power that I hadn't imagined. And, too, these conversations complicated my instincts to impose present-day political assumptions on the past. As with everything else about *Tobe*, the story resists easy answers on the political scorecard. Is *Tobe* a story of exploitation or dignity? Of romanticizing or empowering? Or all of the above?

In the end, my efforts to unspool the layers of history, myth, and reality in *Tobe* blurred the boundaries between all three. The experience of exploring *Tobe* taught me about the enduring power of a story, the resilience of community, and the connection between the two: how a community needs memory to endure. The CSNS/CTI-sponsored discussions extended that lesson into the future: looking back, together, these conversations showed, could create new memories and perhaps foster a new sense of community. Eighty years after Clay McCauley Jr. asked his big question about the power of children's books, new answers continue to resound.

# Book Club Discussion Questions and Essay Overview

*Prior to the event, the planning committee created a list of questions to explore Tobe from three vantage points: text to self, text to text, and text to world.*

**We asked participants to consider the following broad question:**

Do you feel like your stories are told appropriately?

Along with a copy of *Tobe*, additional discussion questions were shared with participants prior to the event:

## Between the Pages

One way to explore a book is to look closely and ask questions about the messages conveyed by its words and images.

- What was your first response to this book? Why?
- Who is speaking in this book? Whose voice do you hear?
- Whose voices would you want to hear if you could invite other characters to speak as alternative narrators?
- What do the words and photographs suggest about the power of work? Of family?
- Do you feel the people in the book are portrayed with dignity or in a romanticized or exploitive way?
- How do you feel the book might have been read differently in 1939 than today? By whom?
- Is this book fiction or nonfiction? What about the book suggests that it is fiction or nonfiction? What is the connection(s) that can be made to fiction or nonfiction?
- What scenes depicted in this book ring true to you as real life? Which seem inauthentic?

- Do you relate to the location of the rural "place" of the story?
- What would you like to know more about relating to this book?

## Beyond the Pages

Another approach to explore a text is to use a book as a point of departure that leads us to broader questions about our own lives and our times.

- What would you want your grandchildren to know about where you live or grew up?
- What was your favorite children's book when you were growing up? Why?
- Why does it matter who appears in our books and media and who tells their stories?
- What might you notice about how African Americans are generally portrayed in books?
- Why do these representations matter for children? For society? How do they persist?
- What would you like to know more about relating to race and representation in media?
- What do you notice about how African Americans and other races/ nationalities/ethnicities are generally portrayed in popular media?

Following the event, participants contributed essays further considering these questions and structuring their thoughts around: the text to self, text to text, and text to world format.

## Participants by Discussion Table (*Essayists Starred)

### TABLE 1

Madge Hopkins, Woodland
  Presbyterian
Naomi ImOberstag, Oakhurst STEAM
  Academy
Janaka Lewis, UNC Charlotte*
Karen Owens, Minister/Chaplain
Jennifer Woods Parker, CMS
  Community
  Partnerships*
Veronica Perry, Crossroad Book Club
Leonard Russ, Grier Heights
  Community
Mary Russ, Grier Heights Community

### TABLE 2

Inez Alexander, CrossRoads Book Study
Kamille Bostick, Levine Museum
Calen Clifton, Martin Luther King Jr.
  Middle School
Venetta DeGraffinried, Billingsville Ele-
  mentary PTA
Jennifer Douglas, PBA Ventures
Regina Gill, Grier Heights Community
Ashli Stokes, UNC Charlotte*

### TABLE 3

Madeline Driscoll, Davidson College
Nellie Holloway-Mixon, Community
  leader
Richard Lancaster, Community Leader*
Ebone Lockett, CATO Middle College
  High
Gregory Mixon, UNC Charlotte
Mike Stewart, CrossRoads Corporation
Jo Stewart, CrossRoads Corporation
Kay Tuttle, The Light Factory

### TABLE 4

Mariem Bchir, Davidson College
Anthony Ellis, UNC Charlotte*
Genora Fant, Grier Heights Presbyterian
Eddie Lynn Finch, Myers Park
  Presbyterian
Maliha Patel, UNC Charlotte
Tara Lynn Sullivan, Central Learning–
  CMS
Gerry Wallace, CMS Central Office
  (retired)

### TABLE 5

Laura Barrett, UNC Charlotte
Avaleen Crawford-Williams,
PriceWaterhouseCoopers
Wendy Kenney, Myers Park
  Presbyterian
Robin Mara, Charlotte Teachers
  Institute
Vivian Mathewson, Grier Heights
  Presbyterian
Danyae Person, Charlotte-Mecklenburg
  Schools
Deanna Stanwood, UNC Charlotte
Jan Swetenburg, The Learning
  Collaborative

### TABLE 6

Micah Cash, The Light Factory*
Kyra Kietrys, Davidson College*
Mary Lou Lindsey, Myers Park
  Presbyterian
Elliott McKenney, UNC Charlotte
Jessica Moss, Harvey B. Gantt Center
Kay Peninger, Charlotte Museum of
  History
Esther Pinto, UNC Charlotte
David Sanders, Grier Heights Presbyte-
  rian Church
Nicole Sparrow, Hawthorne Academy

**TABLE 7**

Cheryl Butler-Brayboy, Johnson C.
Smith*
Scott Gartlan, Charlotte Teachers
Institute*
Ellanor Graves, Ben Salem Presbyterian
Stephanie Misko, Vanguard Group
Barbara Simpson, Grier Heights
Community
Kristine Slade, UNC Charlotte
Debra Smith, UNC Charlotte*
Banu Valladares, NC Humanities
Council

**TABLE 8**

Michelle Beatty, Oakhurst STEAM
Academy
Sara Eudy, UNC Charlotte
Benjamin Filene, UNC Greensboro*
Nancy Gutierrez, UNC Charlotte*
Camay Hunter, West Charlotte High
School
Mae Israel, Community Leader
Deborah Jung, Winding Springs
Elementary*
John McLeod, UNC Press

**TABLE 9**

Eli Davis, Lincoln Heights Academy
Gloria Green, Grier Heights
Community
Tisha Greene, Oakhurst STEAM
Academy*
Diana Leyva, Davidson College
Maria Lignos, UNC Charlotte
Abby Moore, UNC Charlotte
Allen Woodward, Crossroads
Eileen Woodward, Crossroads

# Why *This* Book?

Authorship, Genre, and Reader Reception in *Tobe*

JANAKA B. LEWIS, PH.D. |UNC CHARLOTTE

On Wednesday, April 26, 2017, a group of university and community scholars and members, ranging in ages from 20 plus (and possibly younger) to 70 plus, gathered at the Grier Heights Community Center and at Billingsville Leadership Academy Gym in Charlotte, North Carolina, to discuss the book *Tobe*, authored by Stella Gentry Sharpe in 1939. The group at my lively table, made up of current and former educators, a minister/chaplain, a member of a CMS Community Partnerships, and members of the Grier Heights Community and Crossroad Book Club, had a spirited discussion about the purpose of the book. The words of senior community member and retired educator Madge Hopkins, however, literally rang in my ear: "Well, what did she even write it for?"

Hopkins's poignant question was reminiscent of questions my students in English 2301 (Introduction to African American Literature) had asked weeks earlier when Charlotte Teachers Institute Director Scott Gartlan visited my course to introduce the book and the book club event. "Who was Tobe?" they wanted to know. After reading anthologized course material from the canon of African American literature beginning in the eighteenth century, from genres of nonfiction narrative and memoir to poetry to short and longer fiction, they wondered if this story was about a "real" person.

I didn't have an exact answer at that time, as I was just learning about the text itself. I had learned about the significance of the book, as "one of the first-ever children's books depicting African American life in rural North Carolina." I was interested in its authorship by a white, married woman, in 1939 whose full name, Stella Gentry Sharpe, was listed on the cover. Reading the book in preparation for the club and conversation still didn't answer their question, however. Who *was* Tobe? And, ultimately, weeks later, I was still considering the purpose of the text as I looked for Sharpe's own clues.

As I read the acknowledgments of the text and reread in preparation for the essay, I noted that Tobe was not a direct recipient of his story. Sharpe mentions the former head of the Department of Education at UNC Chapel Hill, Dr. M. R. Trabue, for his encouragement in writing, several members of the faculty and staff at UNC (including the School of Library Science, the Department of Sociology), and her editor Alice T. Paine of the UNC Press. The last dedication, however, mentions the book's photographs. She writes: "to Mr. Charles Farrell, whose photographs have caught the spirit of the text so completely and have made possible the carrying out of a long-delayed plan." After reading those words and hearing the words of the scholar Dr. Benjamin Filene of UNC Greensboro, who explored the significance of the photographed children who were modeled as children and who worked on land owned by Sharpe's family, I wondered even more what that plan was. Was it for Sharpe to be able to circulate the text in the first place, or was she concerned with representing the children in an honest way?

## Text to Self

As contemporary readers and scholars, we might not know the exact answers to these questions, but we can examine the significance of asking them. The central question of the conversation was: "Why does no one in my books look like me?" Although Filene's presentation gave more information on how that life was depicted, and for whom, my tablemate Madge Hopkins's question became even more relevant. If the book was a response to a culture of literature that didn't represent African American faces, but it still limited their experiences in print, was there still work to be done?

Of course, the answer in a contemporary context is yes, but the conversation ranged from whether we should simply appreciate the work that Sharpe had done or push the critique to what she could have done. Thus, the "first responses" ranged from the comments that the book was "pointless," because it didn't represent the characters' truths. We considered the idea, in response to the question: "Whose voices would you want to hear if you could invite other characters to speak as alternative narrators?" That is, we would simply want to hear from the characters themselves. It doesn't matter as much, for some, that the people are portrayed "with dignity," that their experiences are romanticized, or that the narrative poems are matched with images of children whom the stories represent. They/we wanted to know what it would be like to hear the words of those, or those represented, captured by Farrell in photo and Sharpe in text.

## Text to Text

The conversation about voice and representation is one that I also have in my classes. "Does it matter," I often ask, "who is telling the story?" In the case of Harriet Beecher Stowe's *Uncle Tom's Cabin* (1852), written by a white woman about the fictional tales of enslaved Uncle Tom, mother Eliza, child Topsy, and other characters, some might argue that the significance is that the story is told. Stowe's fiction was potentially based on the truth of the many stories that had not necessarily come to light at the time. She was able to give them a platform. What we focus on, however, are the narratives that are told by the authors themselves about their experiences or those of other underrepresented groups or characters. We look at Phillis Wheatley's representation of herself as an "Ethiop" in the 1773 *Poems on Miscellaneous Subjects,* Frederick Douglass's narrative of his enslavement and his escape in his 1845 *Narrative of the Life of Frederick Douglass, An American Slave.* We turn with excitement (at least on my part) to Harriet Jacobs's 1861 *Incidents in the Life of a Slave Girl,* which provokes much interest because it was thought to be fictional with Jacobs using the pseudonym Linda Brent. In the 1980s, scholar Jean Fagan Yellin uncovered more information about this North Carolina author. Further research proved that Jacobs turned to Stowe to help her tell her story but that Stowe wanted to use the story herself. Jacobs, assisted by abolitionist Lydia Maria Child, kept and told her own story.

This information is not to make the argument that one genre (nonfiction or fiction, or even poetry) is better or a more honest representation of experiences. Instead, it is important to ask the question how it matters who is telling the story, especially to that story itself. To make the question more contemporary, we can look at Toni Morrison's first novel, *The Bluest Eye* (1970). Morrison's career as an editor at Random House Publishing brought her attention to a wealth of material—stories, images, primary documents that she collected in *The Black Book.* Her first foray into her own fiction considered a story that was based on ideas of beauty about her own childhood.

In the afterword, Morrison writes about a friend who desired blue eyes:

> We had just started elementary school. She said she wanted blue eyes. I looked around to picture her with them and was violently repelled by what I imagined she would look like if she had her wish. The sorry in her voice seemed to call for sympathy, and I faked it for her, but, astonished by the desecration she proposed, I "got mad" at her instead. (p. 209)

Although Pecola is a fictional character, her story comes from Morrison's very real repulsion that a character who, the reader assumes looks like her, wants something that the author feels she has no right to own or wish for. Morrison continues: "*The Bluest Eye* was my effort to say something about that; to say something about why she had not, or possibly ever would have, the experience of what she possessed and also why she prayed for so radical an alteration" (p. 210).

In providing the narrative about the little girl who was put "outdoors" by her family and taken in by another family, who was raped and impregnated by her father, and abandoned by her mother in favor of a whiter and more pristine life, Morrison had to dig, literally, into her own experiences to provide an honest representation of what the tragedy of Pecola's life would be if her only option, only escape, was to imagine that her eyes were blue and that she was therefore beautiful.

To return to the question at hand, is Sharpe's representation the only "escape" for the fictional Tobe? Are Farrell's photos and Sharpe's words the only ways Tobe and his family (or those like them in rural North Carolina) would have their narratives represented? Possibly, in 1939. Leonard Russ, of the Grier Heights community, talked about the lack of opportunities to even read stories about African Americans when he was growing up. He described the adventure stories he read growing up (including the Hardy Boys series—revised decades later to eliminate racial stereotypes) that only represented white boys. His was the excited voice at the table who noted that he would have been glad to see a book like this. Leonard was quickly interrupted by the chorus from the table, "but this book?" As in, would it have to be this particular book? Or one like it that *did* more?

### Text to World

The question remains—what do we need this book to *do*? What is significant about *this* book that Sharpe wrote and that Farrell's photos helped her realize? I turn, for the answer, to the first entry, "Tobe." It reads: "I am Tobe. / My real

Leonard Russ
discusses the book.

name is Clay Junior. / Tobe is a nickname. / I am six years old. / I go to school. /
We have fun on our farm. / I will tell you about it" (p. 2).

Are the stories about work, about family, about school life, stories that six-
year old Tobe would want to tell, or would he be interested in the adventures
that took place on the farm (like the stories Leonard Russ suggested were popular)? Are the values placed in the text from values that Sharpe and/or Farrell
hold? (Were the conversations, perhaps, about where and how models of characters should be photographed?) The ultimate resolution I (and, I believe, my
table) would argue is that as Sharpe brought her lens to the vision of the text,
we bring our own lenses to the reception of it. We see what is there and try to
imagine what else could be outside of our perspective.

I am Tobe.
My real name is Clay Junior.
Tobe is a nickname.
I am six years old.
I go to school.
We have fun on our farm.
I will tell you about it. (p. 2)

The narrative is accompanied by a picture of a young boy with his finger pointed at the viewer or the reading audience. We learn that this is not actually Tobe, but someone posing for the picture. Perhaps we then question if there is a real Clay Junior, or a Tobe. If so, where does he live? Where is the farm? Where does he go to school? What and how will he tell about it?

We find out, only with additional context, that Tobe is a fictional representation, at least in this book. Although the book comes from a little boy's question, "Why doesn't anyone in my books look like me?"; Tobe doesn't tell his own story (although we hear what could have been his experience). We hear that the stories of Tobe's nine-year-old twin friends Alton and Alvis and five-year-old twins William and Rufus may or may not be true, although there are accompanying images. We learn that Alton and Alvis go to school and William and Rufus don't, since "they help each other work" (and fight). In Tobe's voice, "I do not have a twin to help me," which suggests that he works and/or fights alone (p. 8). We see other family members who could exist through Tobe's eyes—his big sisters Lily Mae, thirteen, and Mary Lee, fourteen, who can "wash, iron, cook, and sew," a suggestion of what life for young women in a rural African American household might be like (p. 13). We learn about the school (they had one, kept "nice and clean"), the animals, the activities (picking peaches), and holidays through the eyes of what could have been a six-year-old boy. The reader ultimately hears the narrative of work, as in "What Brings Good Luck," when Tobe tells his mother how many apples his Aunt Susan had. "She said, 'The horse-shoes did not make the apples grow. Work made them grow. You will have to dig around our trees and spray them.' We did, too. Now we have many apples" (p. 120).

If we have grown up, as the younger generation did, seeing and hearing characters who look like us, we wonder at the stiffness in Tobe's voice (as one of the book club participants did, who argued we do not really hear Tobe's, or even his mother's, voice). If Tobe was our introduction to African American representation in print, we might marvel at the shift in physical representation or wonder if it is honest. Do we receive the spirit of a Tobe or a faux representation altogether?

To return to Madge's question, the answer may be less of determining why *this* book exists by trying to assess Sharpe's intentions and more of what we can learn or see from its existence. The answer may be that we can learn about types of experiences on a farm in North Carolina as told *about* African Americans (by a voice that supposes who they are). Or, it may be that we start to ask the kinds of questions that can't be answered through ventriloquism. Who was the person (or type of person) represented by or as Tobe? Who were his friends? Who were his family members? Where did they live? What was farm life really like? And, finally, what did *he* see?

## References

Douglass, Frederick. (1982). *Narrative of the Life of Frederick Douglass, an American Slave*. New York: Penguin. (Original work published 1845).

Jacobs, Harriet. (2001). *Incidents in the Life of a Slave Girl*. New York: Norton. (Original work published 1861).

Morrison, Toni. (1993). *The Bluest Eye*. New York: Penguin. (Original work published 1970).

Sharpe, Stella Gentry. (1939). *Tobe*. Chapel Hill: UNC Press.

Stowe, Harriet Beecher. (1852). *Uncle Tom's Cabin*. London: J. Cassell,

Wheatley, Phillis. (1989). *Poems of Phillis Wheatley*. Chapel Hill: UNC Press. (Original work published 1773).

# Tobe

## Reflections on Race, Representation, and Identity

JENNIFER WOODS PARKER | CMS COMMUNITY
PARTNERSHIPS AND FAMILY ENGAGEMENT FOR
CHARLOTTE-MECKLENBURG SCHOOLS

In the beginning, I wasn't sure how to pronounce the title. Was it "Toe-bee," like "Toby," a name that works for a boy or a girl? Or was it "To-bay," marked with an accent from above the "e," like a French accessory? It turned out that it was much simpler than that. *Tobe*, we learned at our *Tobe* Community Book Club Experience, is a one-syllable word that rhymes with "globe." Variations in pronunciation were only the beginning of a multitude of opinions we encountered in our discussions at Table 1 about race, representation, and identity, focused through the lens of a children's book first published by the UNC Press in 1939. Problem was, once each of us had etched it in our own minds how to pronounce "Tobe," the name of the book's main character, a six-year-old boy, it was hard to change. Some of us continued with our preferred pronunciations. "I say To-bee," one of us said. No one minded. Throughout the course of the evening we gave one another a gracious plenty in respect and kindness toward the differences among us, whether in pronunciation, interpretation, or experience.

On April 26 when we met, the weather was perfect, but warm for April, more like early summer. Afternoon sun filtered into the Grier Heights Community Center where we gathered for refreshments southern style: hors d'oeuvres, mostly fried, accented with cooked greens and sweet iced tea. We mingled with a variety of participants, community leaders, church members, university professors, and public school teachers who had come to explore race and representation in a setting that has played an important role in the lives of African Americans in Charlotte.

The Grier Heights Community Center once served as a school for the

Guests enjoying the reception.

black community. The building was built at the beginning of the twentieth century through a national program, created by Booker T. Washington and the president of Sears Roebuck, Julius Rosenwald, to educate African American children. After we had shared refreshments and light conversation, we walked across a driveway to the gym of Billingsville Elementary School for our round-table discussions.

For me, the event and the book had a distinctly personal feel. I live not far from the historic black community of Grier Heights and its neighborhood school, Billingsville Elementary. I have tutored students in reading at Billingsville and know people who grew up in the neighborhood. One was a successful high school administrator who told me stories about his childhood in Grier Heights—how he played all day with friends in the fields and countryside, mud squishing between his toes as he looked for frogs and fish in the creek. Women from Grier Heights worked primarily as domestics in Charlotte's finest neighborhoods and men farmed and served as tradesmen—including brick masons and carpenters who built buildings that transformed Charlotte from a regional trading post into a business capital of the New South. As a thoroughly urbanized educator, my administrator friend shared with me a nostalgia for the lifestyle of his childhood—its slower pace and opportunities to explore at will and make your own fun.

Although I grew up in a very different neighborhood in Charlotte, I, too, remembered fondly the days when, as children, we ran freely, left to entertain ourselves while parents worked, kept house, and cooked. I also knew something of the rural life from my mother's large Virginia family who had grown up on a Tidewater farm during the Depression. As a child, I learned to brave gathering the eggs from a henhouse, swung on a rope swing under a sycamore tree, and played in fields that rotated peanuts, soybeans, and cotton for crops.

Initially I was curious about why the book *Tobe* was selected for us to read. Judging from the brown sticker on the cover signaling that it was a UNC Press "Enduring Edition," I guessed it must have some kind of historical importance. It was my kind of book—lots of photos, a large font that made words quick and easy to read, and only 121 pages.

The black-and-white photos drew me in as much as the story. Children wading in a creek with homemade sailboats. The boy Tobe feeding his chickens corn and bread. Boys coddling bolls of cotton in a field of white. My favorite photo is of Tobe's parents sitting by the fireplace —Mother sewing and Daddy listening to the radio—dressed in their Sunday best. Mother sits in a rocking chair, a basket of darning nearby. She pulls a needle through floral fabric, sewing and listening at the same time, not rocking too much. Flowers abound all over this room—on Mother's dress, on the fabric she sews, on the apron she wears, and even on the wallpaper. The scene reminds me of the American Impressionist Mary Cassat whose paintings catch families in the cozy comfort of ordinary moments—a mother bathing her child surrounded by a swirl of patterns on curtains, upholstery, towels, carpets, and clothes. The feeling is pattern on pattern with repeated colors and shapes cocooning us in the reassurance of familiar surroundings and daily routines. As Daddy reads a book by the radio, he leans his ladderback chair on two legs. A round lacy doily drapes across the mantel. Was it tatted by the elderly woman whose photo sits nearby?

Another photo in the book shows *Tobe*'s school, a brick one-story building with tall colonial-style windows that looks like the Grier Heights Community Center where we gathered for our soul food and fellowship. Taking a leap of the imagination, I concluded that the school in the photo must have be the very one we dined in on a pleasant night. I supposed that the professors wanted to teach us about the history of education in Grier Heights and decidedly assumed that all the photos were taken in the early days of Grier Heights when children played in the creeks, squishing mud between their toes. I had a lot to learn.

We gathered at several round tables for a lecture about the author, Stella Gentry Sharpe, a white teacher from Hillsborough, North Carolina. Benjamin Filene, a history professor from UNC Greensboro, explained how the story was written after an African American boy named Clay McCauley, who lived near Sharpe, asked her why there were no books about boys like him. Photographs were taken by a Greensboro newspaper photographer named Charles Farrell. They were not taken in Grier Heights at all, but in Goshen, an African American town near Greensboro (Blythe, 2012). I had even more to learn from our discussion.

## Text to Self: Our Table's Reaction to Tobe

Our table was facilitated by UNC Charlotte Professor Janaka Lewis, who opened our book discussion by asking us: "What was your first response and why?" Answers varied greatly from, "What's the point?" to "My thought was that it was elementary," to "Initially, I thought it was a good children's book—it took me to places I had been." Madge Hopkins of Woodland Presbyterian Church was the first to speak: "My first response was, 'What's the point?' Growing up in the rural south about this time, . . . I thought it [the book] was really simplistic. There was no struggle. Life was so glorious and beautiful, and it [real life] wasn't like that. . . ." Grier Heights Community Member Mary Russ said, "I guess I came from a different perspective because all I could think was [the book] *Dick and Jane*. See Dick run. See Spot, and this book to me was little bit more . . . profound. The way they went through and told about the little boy, it could be taught all year long, and [back then] it wasn't allowed."

Whose *voice* did we hear in the story? Mary Russ heard the author's voice—in proper English, clarifying, "It just wasn't the voice of a child." First-grade teacher Naomi ImOberstag agreed that she did not hear the real voice of a child either: "These are things we want to hear," she said. Hopkins heard in the narrative a mother's voice observing things in an idealistic way. She emphasized that for her, not hearing the authentic voice of a young boy was problematic. If she were to address the narrator in the story, she would say: "You do *not* know my story." Hopkins pointed out some important omissions in the book. She felt that the narrator's voice silenced the realities of the struggles and difficulties endured by African Americans during this time. "That world wasn't beautiful. That world was filled with conflict. When I walked down the road to the school bus and things that were hurled at me were offensive. . . . I think that I resented the book." Leonard Russ, a Grier Heights Community member and the husband of Mary Russ, felt differently: "But without this book, this discussion would not take place." He suggested that depending on whether you took the perspective of *then* or you took the perspective of *now*, the book is two different books. Thinking of the book's audience *then* and the book's audience *now* led some to wonder how their grandchildren would respond to this story.

Our facilitator said we had segued into her next questions and asked us to consider *who* we thought this book was written for in 1939? Who was the audience then? And how might it be read differently today? There was general consensus that the book was written for the boy who had asked why there were no books about children like him.

Leonard Russ acknowledged the author, Stella Gentry Sharpe, for her initiative: "That was a noble effort on her part in that day and age in North Carolina . . . as a black, I said, 'High Five—(even though parts of the book were) imaginary . . . and all of that, because the world was a different place. . . . He concluded: "It was laudable." Mary Russ highlighted some of the images that resonated for her—a description of washing clothes and a snake that got in Tobe's way on the road to his Aunt Mary's house. She laughed and wanted to ask Tobe: "Why didn't you go around it?" Hopkins pushed our questioning deeper, challenging the relevance of *Tobe* for today's world: "Our children being African American are experiencing something much worse than this (the lives depicted in the book). Inequality. Murder. So many other things that keep our children from achieving and living a good life." Our group honored the point. Perhaps in those days in some ways, life was simpler, better. "We were raised by a village," said Mary Russ. Veronica Perry, a member of the Crossroads Book Club, echoed the sentiment: "A child was everyone's child."

We were asked to consider what in the book rang true to us. Mary Russ highlighted the plum trees and blackberry bushes. "Were things this nice?" wondered Leonard Russ. "I had to say (to myself): "Stop Leonard—there were black farmers (in those days) who were well off. They had respect. They were landowners. . . . They were some of the kids in our classes. We were also blessed because they were there with us." A former teacher, he reflected on the importance and effectiveness of his own teachers, both inside and outside the classroom. He said he especially treasured all he learned from the friends and families—rich and poor—he grew up with. He and his friends were learning both "when we were in classes, but also in the woods playing." He continued: "It was not just what my parents gave me, but what *other* parents gave us."

His memories of visiting the homes of friends who had less than he included learning to enjoy oatmeal when there wasn't much else to eat and seeing how people killed chickens in order to cook them for dinner. He expressed great gratitude for the community in which he grew up. "We were surrounded by good things, by black people who were nurturing, teaching, feeding, sharing," he recollected. During the times of civil rights and unrest, he felt that all along he was grounded by the people around him. "Some of those things (civil rights violence and unrest) did not shake us because we returned to the cocoon of nurture and safety."

Lewis then asked us to think about what *cannot* be known by the story. What might be happening that we could not see behind the scenes. What was left out? "What's missing for me—" said Hopkins, "there's no color in the book. . . . Children think and write with color. They're technicolored. This is all black and white. A simple sentence, a subject, a verb. . . .'" She felt the style and voice showed an absence of creativity that ignored the tremendous contributions African Americans have made to so many art forms, especially music and dance.

"I hear you, but I don't feel the same," said Leonard Russ. "If you were living in that day and age, you could almost see the colors if you closed your eyes. . . . As a boy who lived in the woods and played in the woods, as I lived with them as I reread the story the third time, I saw colors . . . whole bunches of colors," he said.

Lewis asked, Were we talking about colors of objects or colors of people? Was there an effort to try to universalize the people? Leonard Russ ventured further: "A picture is worth a thousand words. But at the same time, it hit me that—deep dark black kids—did I see them? I had to look at those pictures a second time. And as part of the culture and what was acceptable . . . you had to be sort of light skinned. But I wouldn't hold that against the book. I would hold that against the society." I told the group about the high school administrator I knew who grew up in Grier Heights, and how the book made me think of him as a boy playing outdoors. Several group members knew him, too.

As we expanded on themes of color, Perry remembered her great-grandmother's grand arch with roses. Hodges remembered her grandmother's dahlias. And we recalled the books we had loved best when we were children—*Dick and Jane, Boys Life Magazine,* and *Treasure Island.* Our memories of beautiful things and cherished books pointed to a deeper, often unspoken truth.

## Text to Text: *Tobe* and Other Books of the Era

Not a single one of the books loved by an African American at our table featured a black person or came from black cultural heritage. Every book was produced by and for the white culture that predominated in the 1940s and 1950s. "There was an absence of books with people who look like us," said Leonard Russ. Participants talked about the ongoing difficulty of finding books by African American authors for their grandchildren. "We might have been robbed," he added.

A cascade of memories followed: Front of the bus/back of the bus. Eating/not eating at the Woolworth lunch counter. Separate water fountains. Segregated restrooms. Girls disqualified from becoming majorettes because their skin was too dark. Some who lived through segregation shared that they had felt powerless to change things. It was just the way things were. Others said they followed the rules but refused to accept them.

Lewis posed our final question: "Why do these representations matter (or not) for children." "I think it matters because we have not reached true equality," Mary Russ said. Lewis said she recently wrote a children's book for her son titled *Brown All Over* because the scarcity of children's literature about and by African Americans continues.

## Text to World: Does *Tobe* Resonate in Today's World?

Children talk about skin color. Someone recalled a grandchild describing skin color by using the names of ice cream—blends of chocolate and vanilla. Another recalled a child asking about another child, "Does he look like me?"

The heart of the matter emerged as we shared our last thoughts. We want children to be proud of who they are. We see the need to discover positive representations while still telling the truth. All this can create challenges for today's children, families, educators, and communities.

As leaders announced that the end of our time was near, Hopkins pointed to the world awaiting us: "Where do we go from this experience?"

Lewis asked if we thought the people and stories portrayed in *Tobe* were relatable today. Perry responded: "I think they were portrayed with dignity." Long after the Grier Heights Book Club Experience ended, I read a blog from the UNC Library about *Tobe*. Two responses intrigued me. They told very different stories.

One was from Charles Watkins, the nephew of Charles "Windy" Garner who as a child had posed for the photos of the boy, Tobe. He wrote:

> I'd like there to be illumination on the important contributions (and sacrifice) that the Garner family made. Aside from opening up their family to this project, my grandfather initiated litigation against Charles Farrelll (sic) the photographer, regarding lack of full compensation for the use of the images. As you might suspect, a black man suing a white man in 1940's North Carolina was not without several risks. That story and the making of Tobe can be found in great detail in Charles Farrell's papers which were donated to, and reside in the UNC Chapel Hill Library Collections. (Blythe, 2012)

Another response to the blog came from Sue Dodson who had been tutored by Tobe's author, Stella Gentry Sharpe. She wrote:

> I grew up knowing Stella and Luther Sharpe. Into her eighties she tutored children, helping us with math, reading and homework. She taught me fractions between second and third grade. She told me that Tobe and Tilde were children close to where she grew up. She grew up in the North Carolina Mountains. She had Alzhiemer's and died in Mrs. Yancy's nursing home on Main street in Hillsborough. I loved her dearly and still miss her.
> (Sue Dodson, February 28, 2016)

The book Tobe did not end discrimination and segregation in the South. The writing of Stella Gentry Sharpe and photographs of Charles Farrell tell a made-up story from an outsider's perspective. Tobe presents us with images too pretty to be real. Nonetheless, despite constraints of race, gender, and politics, Sharpe took a significant step by refusing to ignore a child. She honored that child's question, answering it in the best way she could through the book Tobe. Tobe offers a narrow and dated vision, to be sure. But it is not inconsequential that some eighty years later, Tobe brought together a group of strangers and inspired them to share experiences, disappointments and dreams, showing in black and white that the truth belongs to all.

## References

Blythe, John. (2012, October 24). "The Story Behind the Children's Book Tobe," in *North Carolina Miscellany: Exploring the History, Literature, and Culture of the Tar Heel State.* Retrieved from http://blogs.lib.undu/ncm/index.php/2012/10/24/the-story-behind-the-childrens-book-tobe/.

# Tobe or To Be

A Good and Noble Idea Meets Rural Realities in
1930s North Carolina

RICHARD A. LANCASTER | CHARLOTTE COMMUNITY LEADER

**W**hy does no one in my books look like me?," asked by an eight-year-old young boy in rural North Carolina of his teacher. The young boy is a Negro (term of the day) and the teacher is a white woman, who is very sympathetic to the young boy's piercing question. Thus began the teacher's quest to produce a work that would have African American characters as the main subjects. A very decent and noble response to the simple but profound question asked by the young boy. As the teacher creates the story, she identifies the main character, a young eight-year-old Negro boy named Tobe. While I have heard many pronunciations of the name, I wondered and I believe the teacher intended for the name would be pronounced as To Be, as in I exist. I believe her attempt at addressing the young boy's painful observation was pure, designed to promote the young boy's self-esteem, and seeking only the best results. The name considered as "To Be," I believe, represented the best of her intentions.

In our review of this book and background story, we learned that at the time the book was put together the young boy would have grown to high school age. Therefore, he could no longer be represented as a child. The teacher hired a photographer who found willing candidates to portray the story using a younger boy as To Be. They proceeded to have several photo shoots for the book. The pictures depicted various phases of the daily life of To Be. The pictures were staged with African American characters and the story line pursued of what some have deemed to be something less than a real representation of rural African American life in 1930s North Carolina. One needs to keep in mind that this is a children's story, with the primary intended audience of young African American children.

The story is in an idyllic setting where To Be interacts with family and friends. It describes various family members playing, working, and living in the rural North Carolina countryside. The descriptions of the characters and their roles in the family lead one to believe that To Be had a very stable and normal childhood, with loving parents who were hard working and prosperous. One got the sense that To Be's family was in complete control of their circumstances and that they were thriving in the waning days of Depression-era America. Many scenes involved various acts of play with family and friends. Neatly dressed children played in the outdoors and seemed to avoid ever ruffling or soiling their clothes. Adults were depicted as industrious and in pursuit of all manners of self-development. The interaction with the outside world typically went without any discernable incident.

Given this brief introduction to the origins of the book and some of the events that occur in bringing the story to life, I would like to address several questions that arose when I introduced the book to several of my family members who come in a range of generations, genders, and perspectives. When I did this, it was very interesting to view their reactions and perspectives about the story and the author's intentions. Hopefully the questions that I pose will provide some perspective and understanding about how complex it is when a person of one race attempts to tell the story of the person of another race. Surely there are more questions that could be addressed and I invite you to raise those to further gain a better understanding of this issue.

### Text to Self: Who owned the story—the teacher or the student? Who should benefit from any financial gain created by the story?

I asked this question of family members who represented different generations. It was interesting to me that at least one baby boomer and millennial shared the same opinion: the *author owned the story and that the subject had no rights to the story*. In general, the other millennials I asked thought differently, and I share their view. To Be is, in my view, too young to have the capacity to negotiate the question of ownership. It was his longing for an answer that motivated the teacher to create the book and the story. While I do not think that he is entitled to something approaching 50 percent, I do not think his share is zero either. For me, this issue has some bearing on the story and its resulting impact. I feel that the story began with a noble and honorable effort that somehow was

Richard Lancaster
discusses his group's
observations.

corrupted by the elements of the time (southern, rural North Carolina in the
1930s America where blacks did not have anything close to an equal standing in
the society), and the relative positions each party held in the community. For
To Be, to be locked out of any economic benefits that were derived from this
effort represents another example of the dominant culture benefitting from
the minority culture at their expense. I believe the teacher's intentions were
pure in trying to respond to To Be's question. I would have been thoroughly
convinced that she was as interested in To Be's overall development had she
included him in on any of the economic or financial gains that resulted from
the creation of this story.

### Text to Text: What was the purpose of telling the story as if the family had no concerns common to rural southern African Americans at that time in our country's history?

The connection to historical reality is what caused the greatest feeling of anxiousness on my part. I am used to early movies like *Sounder* and the *Learning Tree* where young African Americans faced life's challenges in their effort to reach their full potential. Invariably some figure from the dominant white culture interjects themselves in the story to exercise their privilege that results in some negative consequences or outcomes for the young black protagonist. This story had none of that possibility to its credit. We must keep in mind the teacher's original mission: responding to To Be's initial question concerning the lack of relatable characters. Furthermore, the audience for this book was young children. How many of the stories directed toward our youth err on the overly positive side? It was and is not uncommon to omit what would be an essential detail in a work directed toward a young audience.

### Did the story ultimately address To Be's original question in a positive way?

In my view, one would be hard pressed to argue that the book did not achieve its objective. It told To Be's story. The characters were young people like him and he would have recognized them. It was interesting that in our focus group a couple of members grew up with the book and remember it fondly. A point my daughter made bears some consideration, as she warned that we need to consider the standards and criteria used when white authors write about black experiences. She also suggested considering who the primary audience is for a children's book: those attending predominantly white schools or those attending predominantly black ones. On one hand, the book presents positive images of black people with whom whites may not have been familiar. On the other hand, the story could be received negatively, if black children were aware enough to know that representation was not part of any world they had seen or with which they were familiar. My son raised an interesting point directed toward the critics of Sharpe's representation. If you questioned whether the story achieved its objective, then be consistent in your criticism of other blacks who aren't attempting to respond positively to recognized deficits in the black community, such as the lack of support of black-owned enterprises by black customers. Why criticize the effort in creating the book and not be critical of a lack of effort for the other? Consistency was an important crite-rion from his point of view.

### Text to World: Is it important to present the complete picture while responding to To Be's original request?

As a children's story, probably not. As a young adult's story, definitely so. How soon should we open the eyes of children to the real world? When is the ap-propriate age or time to introduce the complexities that exist? From my point of view, I thought it very odd that this family had little or no contact with the greater world. I appreciated the fact that the families' standing was somewhat elevated, but think the book conveyed a false sense of social progress.

One item deserves consideration. The teacher's husband owned the land where To Be's family were sharecroppers. This fact injects an element to the story that further complicates the author's motives and outcomes. Was her response from a sense of guilt? Perhaps the prevailing social and economic climate of that time had an impact that detracted from the author's original intention.

Is this a story that has some relevance in today's world?

This book represents the result of one person in a closed community address-ing the concerns of a young man. It was written in earlier days of literature, performing arts, theater, and motion pictures that depicted blacks in all types of circumstances. For the most part, blacks were usually represented in less than flattering ways and portrayals tended to be more stereotypical than realis-tic. This story has relevance because it deals with the daily actions of children. There are some themes and conflicts that are universal and timeless. I suggest that the book has some relevance to telling the stories of African Americans, but is limited by the concerns discussed throughout this essay.

I believe this book was a noble and genuine attempt to respond to the trou-blesome and indicting question of a young black boy in 1930s North Carolina. Something happened along the way, the environment and racial climate of the South in general and the state in peculiar, that could not help but interfere and alter the true and pure motives behind this work.

# The Search for Identity

Exploring Representations of Black Culture through *Tobe*

ANTHONY ELLIS | UNC CHARLOTTE STUDENT

Developing a conceptual understanding of Stella Gentry Sharpe's book *Tobe* provides many audiences with a unique perspective of the text's true meaning. Sharpe presents the story of a six-year old boy Tobe through his daily journey, introducing other influential figures such as his immediate family, along with including the stories that guided his thought process. Each person introduced, story depicted, and lesson learned enables readers to obtain a window into Tobe's mindset and his family's lifestyle. The further introduction of essential childhood memories presents viewers with an innate sense of authenticity in the vision Sharpe shares.

Our table discussion focused collectively on the stories shared from Tobe's perspective in terms of how they documented the experience of black culture, elicited excitement in African American dialect of the era, and created a sense of authenticity in the narrator's voice. Many participants developed a positive outlook of the story while also exuding a critical response regarding how they did not have the opportunity to read a text such as this early age. The importance of depicting underrepresented groups such as Tobe's family helped to shine a light on the lack of diversified novels in early education while prompting action steps to rectify such concerns. As a current college student, it was my role to shine a light on key issues relating to race and representation through literature from work explored in recent years. One such issue includes examining how the author's portrayal of the family ultimately corresponds or contradicts preexisting norms of black culture in the 1930s. Our discussion on race, representation, and identity showed how far society must go to improve conditions while acknowledging the potential that using tools in literature can have. The generational impacts of allowing for new forms of literature could alter the portrayal of "real life" as it was in 1939.

Various groups discussing *Tobe*.

## Text to Self

When initially reading the book, I felt as though I gained an exclusive depiction of black life during a period that did not previously offer as much from a personal narrative perspective. A novel that told the story of children of color growing up on a farm (a story I have often heard from my grandfather and uncle's experiences) was a new perspective that excited me. When I was growing up, reading literature adhered to a standard protocol and yielded similar storylines as a result. Having the opportunity to read noteworthy classics like *Fahrenheit 451, The Adventures of Huckleberry Finn, To Kill a Mockingbird,* and *Animal Farm* were essential for my early development but also limiting because they omitted certain perspectives. The contextualization of *Tobe* spoke volumes due to the "realness" in how he describes his family and the traits they share. For example, the representation of his mother and daddy as going to church on Sundays while describing their duties of farming and canning food recognizes their responsibilities in a manner that readers can understand as well as relate to themselves. Immediately, from the initial five to fifteen pages of the text, I could connect on a personal level with Tobe, which helped to allow for a greater appreciation for his later tales.

Another initial reaction to the book was how influential the mother was in providing the children with essential life lessons through their daily activities, including working on the farm and simultaneously allowing them to receive as many rewarding childhood experiences as possible. The representation of the mother as the family's stalwart figure corresponds to not only my personal experience as a child with a strong parent leading their family but also with that of others. The mother's nurturing mindset is shown in how she provides the children with a Christmas surprise to meet Santa Claus who rides in an automobile to deliver the children's presents. The surprise came after the children finished many of their labor-intensive tasks including cleaning the yard, carrying wood, milking the cow, and feeding the pigs. In response to their challenging work, the mother (with daddy's assistance) essentially rewards them in a manner that offers each child a lifelong memory. The mother's presence stuck out during my initial reading and emerged as a key talking point during various parts of our group discussion. The story of Christmas connected greatly to me because I remember the importance of that holiday from my upbringing. As a young child having the chance to meet Santa Claus makes a seamless connection to Tobe through this memory. One untold story is the mother's ability to maintain strong relations with every individual in the family while balancing their seemingly immense economic stresses along the way. Her voice, as expressed through Tobe's dialogue, allowed for many characterizations that allow readers to romanticize respectfully the daily challenges she endures to keep the family afloat.

How we as a culture view Tobe's life delves into whether people in the book are portrayed with dignity or in a romanticized or potentially exploitative way. For me, the presentation of the mother and father shows a unit that is both hard working and caring while simultaneously understanding of the stresses of the time in raising a family. This book allows the nobility of the family unit to gain prominence among a diverse audience. The definition of how families have evolved over time relates to how those outside of family units react as well. The "village concept" of the book connects with what Gerry Wallace (CMS Central Office) described as most blacks incorporating community members to play a part in raising children and helping out in this era. The closeness of community reflected in Tobe personified a common view in how influential his cousins and others were in his development. Often, how individuals in a community identity themselves in relation to their families plays a vital role in their response to that family's continued development. As the value of personal responsibility and freedom has increased, a sense of shared responsibility for the neighborhood child down the street has been lost, especially in the black community, because it is no longer contextualized as vital to the development of successful families. Mutual feelings of appreciation regarding neighbors and communities could slowly but surely rebound if given the opportunity to explore our history in literature from a perspective that they had not heard from prior.

The process of formulating coherent feelings about identity emerges in the text through Tobe's narration of life from his vantage point. When reading the book, it appeared as though he was inviting the audience to gain a window into his daily life, where he might have at first been apprehensive but gained confidence due to his parents' lessons. Through the stories of "My Garden," Thanksgiving," "Time at the Mill," and others it was abundantly clear that Tobe hoped to provide as many perspectives of his life as possible so the audience could gain an understanding into his life. The incorporation of various anecdotes provided more credence because he shared insights of struggle instead of singularly focusing on the fun times shared with his siblings, friends, and cousins. By including the arduous work of picking cotton and harvesting sweet potatoes, for example, Tobe allows me a window into his thought process of what is normal, in addition to necessary, for his family to continue daily.

### Text to Text: Reading *Tobe* Then and Now

Exploring the participant's initial thoughts after reading the text offered key insights into the multiplicative nature of the book's messages. In our group, only Genora Fant, a member of Grier Heights Presbyterian Church, had the opportunity to read the book while in elementary school, where she pronounced the main character's name as "Tobey." After rereading the book, Fant firmly acknowledged the powerful sense of the family unit. Her perspective was impressive to other group members including Wallace, who gained a keen apperception for the story while also questioning the importance of reading the book. Wallace referenced the childhood tale of *Dick and Jane,* by William S. Gray and Zerna Sharp, which emerged as a key talking point because that book was what she and others read at any early education level. Despite that book's ubiquity, *Tobe* seemed to be the answer to the flaws of books from that era. From Wallace's perspective, exposing black and white children alike to *Tobe* could have created dialogue about the lifestyles of many black southerners.

The lack of stories that incorporate diverse outlooks led our group to yearn for more *Tobe*-style tales. The importance of this book in showing a family unit in the black community that presented love and care would have been essential for all young children to learn about. The correction of potentially disingenuous and objectionable media portraits relating to the black household offer an opening for books such as this to gain prominence. Additionally, the educational value of the story documenting the discipline of farming and other activities presents an almost middle-class portrayal of a lower-class family. The importance of the family growing their own food, taking it to the market, and preparing it from scratch, such as the example of making candy from maple syrup, displays an entrepreneurship that did not readily exist in literature regarding black culture in that period. The abundant learning opportunities presented in the text, even for college-students such as myself and other adults in our group, are invaluable.

The theme of family in black culture, in conjunction with the easy readability of the text, provides another point for why these types of books should appear in early education classrooms. Discussion of the representation of characters led to how black children at any early age might have felt potentially lesser of themselves because they did not have a text such as *Tobe*. Conveying black family unit(s) in a positive light combats otherwise negative stereotypes or caricatures that manifest in society, especially in the South. The question "why don't I see people like me in books?" is an important one that had gone unanswered for many black students growing up in a society whose literature presented a sort of happy-go-lucky characterization of life. Eddie Lynn Finch's (Myers Park Presbyterian Church) experience as a ninth-grade English teacher in Atlanta, for example, who taught three black students who transferred in from other areas, provided her with an additional sense of why texts such as *Tobe* are so important to black students. Her transfer students were not accepted fully by their classmates in school.

Nevertheless, while analyzing the voice of the book, Maliha Patel (UNC Charlotte) introduced the point of why it would be important to hear from Tobe's siblings, and especially his sisters, since female characters often lacked a voice or detailed portrayal in comparison to their male counterparts. Having the opportunity to hear the rich narration of his sisters' stories and experiences would be tremendous since they have an underdeveloped voice. The female characters were described as cooking food, picking flowers, and ironing clothes, which despite the innovative nature of the book, continues a regressive view of women's roles. The simplicity in the text regarding Tobe's life, however, simply allowed some in the discussion to conclude he had a good life without experiencing the complexities of adulthood.

I believe the "voice" of Tobe shifts outward to other characters at various points since he wants to offer a window toward their thought process for the traits that describe them. When discussing his sisters, he says they help their mother in the summer as a way of showing that they feature a similar shared responsibility that he has toward helping his parents. The decision of the author to provide Tobe as a singular voice led many in our discussion to feel it would be informative to hear other perspectives like the mother's, since she was so well respected and had different relationships with the other characters. Hearing how she balanced her daily responsibilities in conjunction with maintaining a strong relationship with her working husband, along with the children, would have been enlightening to the audience. Gaining her perspective about how Tobe acted as a child would have also created a secondary perspective of his development. Reflectively, the discussion of identity among minority women emerges in prominence because the characterization of the mother as an all-knowing liaison for knowledge only paints one portrait of her skillset. Learning about her hobbies, what makes her happy, disappointed, and how her future ambitions clash with her current life, are all features missing in the narration of the story. Nonetheless, the "voice" does allow for intellectual growth and stimulation while maintaining a keen sense of authenticity.

The photographs in the book do an effective job of suggesting the power of work and family through various lenses. Tobe, in his many iterations of work and play, offers a roadmap to early development while adhering to family responsibilities. His journey is not offered through the viewpoint of how children grow up today, which in turn makes his portrayal even more telling. Photographs from Charles Farrell tell a new and powerful story of how work can join groups of people together toward a common goal. Knowledge provided to the audience through images can capture larger lessons because it allows a story to become contextualized. The photographs are essential because it is important for minority children to see themselves depicted on a grand scale. All literature documents shared experiences. The pictures of Tobe completing tasks for his parents provide an authenticity but also a sense of disbelief when comparing contemporary life to this period. The tasks asked of Tobe and his siblings almost seem unrealistic because they are now expected only of adults, such as picking tobacco and working at the mill. On one hand, it is gives the impression that Tobe is happy with a lifestyle that today would be potentially illegal and violate child labor laws. Maybe this thought process is the manifestation of privilege from a young adult speaking in 2017 who has rarely worked outside in the field, but the representation of Tobe's tasks almost makes me feel as though he does not know what's best for him.

An emerging theme throughout the discussion of the text was the importance and significance of shoes. Charles Farrell's photographs offer a keen visual portrayal of Tobe with bare feet while playing with his siblings, feeding the chickens, and at many other times. Even when working outside, the book pictures Tobe without shoes alongside his siblings. The images of Tobe without shoes simply made Fant want him to put on shoes for his own good. To her, shoes symbolized a protection that was necessary for him when working in difficult conditions. Meanwhile, from Finch's perspective, Tobe simply made a personal choice, exhibiting how the story creates many interpretations. For some during the conversation, the idea of wearing nice shoes to play and do outside work was unnecessary, since shoes were saved for special occasions. Additionally, Fant and Wallace described how families frequently had to share shoes with other siblings and tended to receive hand-me-downs that might be worn out or not in pristine shape. These stories offer an interesting connection back to Tobe's character with which audiences can connect. The effect of hand-me-down textbooks in schools is one such connection. During segregation, it was common for black schools to get the used textbooks from white schools (with fiscal responsibility cited as the reason).

## Text to World

For today's young Americans, reading the text could have an enormous influence on fostering a discussion of race, identity, and culture while featuring an underrepresented group. Today, many children grow up in communities that feature individuals of all sorts of races, religions, and nationalities. The presentation of a culturally rich black family growing up with distinct challenges could unite children of all colors and allow them to relate collectively to the characters as the story progresses. The lessons gained from Tobe and his siblings connect over seventy years later to children today. The tin box story of how Tobe deals with the older bully has connections to those growing up now as well. His mother's advice to bring the tin box with pepper as an attempt to scare away the bully reflects upon the challenge some young children have in standing up to those who impede their ability to learn and develop relationships essential for their growth. In that moment, Tobe was not simply standing up for himself, but also developing the ability to problem solve in a nonviolent manner. This teaching point and additional stories about the value of taking responsibility assist and inspire other young children. Another prominent lesson gained from telling this story that repeatedly emerged in our group discussion is the importance of community and the family unit. Black culture, even today, emphasizes family reunions and older generations sharing stories that have meaning with new generations. The stories told provide young adults like myself with experiences that cannot replicate themselves in practice but will likely emerge through alternative means in future endeavors. Manifestations of family unity go beyond race to capture how such togetherness can make an everlasting difference. Children's literature in the twenty-first century has the challenge of presenting a diverse grasp of society while portraying the remnants of individuals' pasts. Coming together to teach history from this perspective will provide greater depth and power to children. The rich culture shared here and told elsewhere of our past creates the urgency for children to read texts that lack societal stereotypes and instead enables forward-looking knowledge and simultaneous growth.

# Illustration or Documentation?

MICAH CASH | DIRECTOR OF COMMUNITY ENGAGEMENT,
THE LIGHT FACTORY

Photography is one of the few mechanical processes that can both replicate and interpret simultaneously. Historically, photography is a means of establishing record: important events, important people, and important places. In this regard, a camera is nothing more than a tool that creates an image with the assumption that anything we see within it is inherently true. Forensic photography, photojournalism, and nature photography all build on the trust that we place within both a single image and the process that created it. Yet photography captures more than detail. It also has the power to interpret what is being seen and to create images with meaning, mood, and narrative. Suddenly the camera is not simply a tool for replication, but a means for photographers to look through their viewfinders with wonder or bias. With a camera in hand, one can not only look at a subject, but also control how others should look at the same subject. Photographers have absolute control over the details of what story is being told, and the pillars of the medium provide this influence: light, composition, value, and focus. What is included in the frame? How is the subject being portrayed? What does the photographer want me to look at? In this regard, photography has the power to present more questions than answers.

As I reflect upon the *Tobe* Book Club Experience, I feel that we neglected to consider the photographs as central components of Stella Gentry Sharpe's book. They were, of course, brought up in conversation, but we failed to consider them as illustrations. Appropriate conversations about authenticity, privilege, and representation swirled throughout the room, but the role that Charles Farrell's sixty-one photographs played within our reading of the book was absent. As we respond to and, potentially, teach this book eight decades after it was written, it is important to have an equal discussion about Farrell's photographs and what information is specifically portrayed through them.

Photographs in the hallway at Grier Heights Community Center/Billingsville Rosenwald School.

## Text to Self: What is and isn't in the photographs?

Most important, there is no mention of the protagonist as being African American. Instead, this information is relayed to the reader solely through the imagery. Page one emphasizes how important the photographs were to Sharpe, as she wrote (as a third-person narrator), "This is Tobe and his brothers." The consideration of the paired photograph is clear, and she reinforces this emphasis by ending the page with, "Can you find him?" We are specifically told to look at the photograph. Reading the image beyond the consideration of race, we can see that all the boys are dressed similarly, five of the brothers are sitting on a wagon, all but one of them are smiling, and some are not wearing shoes. This establishes that they live on a farm as the text tells us and that they are all relatively happy. In this instance, the photograph does exactly what it was intended to do: establish the race of the protagonist and his family and situate them within the setting of a farm. This first page proves that Farrell's photography is successful in terms of intention, which was twofold: to provide a children's book with a protagonist that looked like Clay McCauley Jr. and to illustrate the author's text. Indeed, the photographs successfully illustrate Sharpe's story throughout the book. The images are well composed, warm, and often humorous. They present agrarian life as hard work colored by moments of levity, wonder, and occasional adversity.

Since Farrell's photographs used models rather than McCauley Jr. and his family, he had the freedom to construct vignettes, giving him complete control in terms of composition and tone and making it easier to pair imagery to specific situations. The images portray an agrarian lifestyle in terms of setting, tools, clothing, and chores. For instance, the two images illustrating "Our Cart" (p. 43–44) show boys at play, while "Helping Daddy" (p. 74) and "Turning the Grindstone" (p. 85) illustrate physical labor. While Farrell's images succeed in both instances, we must remember that they are illustrations rather than documentary photographs. Farrell did not photograph a family of sharecroppers in the act of working, instead he used models to depict the text. Even photographs such as "Our School" (p. 17) and "Our Church" (p. 19) should not be approached as social documentation. Yet that does not mean that they do not have historical merit. As members of my table attested, these photographs did represent a life they remembered, and they captured a narrative that was truthful. However, as one of our discussants cautioned, they did not tell the entire truth. David Sanders, a member of nearby Grier Heights Presbyterian Church, who grew up on a farm and recognized much of the imagery as true to life, was quick to point out that the book and its photographs managed to leave out much of the unpleasant qualities of farm life. For example, when Tobe mentions his dislike of an activity, the discussion of that chore, such as picking cotton on page 58, is pivoted to mention its merits and necessity. This underscores a topic that consumed most of our conversation at Table 6 during the *Tobe* experience: privilege.

### Text to text: Connections to images of the era

When we learned that Clay McCauley Jr.'s family were sharecroppers on the author's farm, we began to see the text in a different light. This knowledge colors the relationship of the author to MCauley Jr. and possibly explains why he felt comfortable asking her why there were no children's books with boys that looked like him, as well as to why she might want to write one. It also suggests that the reason there is no discussion about agrarian hardship or the difficult circumstances of the chores, is that she, the author, had never experienced them since she was the landowner and not a landworker. Indeed, I believe that one of the most puzzling occurrences in the book is the switch from third-person to first-person point of view on page 2. I do not want to speculate as to why Sharpe chose to put her voice first and Tobe's second, but I read it as one of authority. It is proclaimed from a privileged position—that she knows Tobe and his family, thus everything that follows is true.

The perceived documentary nature of Farrell's photographs is due to when they were made and their overall pictorial style. They share a similar tonality and composition to photographs that were commissioned by the Farm Security Administration (FSA) in the late 1930s and as such have much in common with the most proliferated images from that New Deal program. Images such as "Raeford" (p. 5) and "Mother and Daddy" (p. 11) present a mix of portraiture and environment. While imagery by photographers such as Walker Evans and Dorothea Lange come to mind, it is important to remember that FSA photography was intended to document impoverished sharecropper communities. Farrell's photographs, however, never explicitly illustrate poverty: clothing does not appear worn, farm equipment is well-maintained, and Tobe's house is furnished. While I appreciate that Tobe and his family are not portrayed as poor sharecroppers, this certainly emphasizes the staged nature of the photographs in the book. If these were true documentary images, I would expect to see some dirt on the boys' hands and clothing, and at the very least, perhaps some sweat on their brows. I would also expect them to be wearing shoes, a detail that I find extremely problematic. All of this staging leads me categorize these photographs as illustrations. They are constructed tableaus meant to simulate farm life rather than truly capture it. While that categorization might seem negative, I do not mean it in a critical fashion. That was the task Charles Farrell was commissioned to undertake, and one in which he succeeded.

## Text to World:
## What do the photographs mean in contemporary life?

I would argue that the photographs are more important to *Tobe* than the text, but they lose meaning without it. We cannot properly consider or critique them in a vacuum as their inclusion within the book is a direct response to Clay McCauley Jr.'s inquiry. While the images are stylized and occasionally romantic, they go to great lengths to normalize African American farm life. Yet they also neglect its hardships, avoid overt imagery of poverty, and gloss over the violent and oppressive history of racial segregation and Jim Crow. These disconcerting omissions should absolutely be discussed when teaching this book. Contemporary discourse about representation and authenticity should be woven into our discussion, but I also believe that we must consider the initial intention. Stella Gentry Sharpe chose to use photography in her book rather than traditional graphic illustrations, and Charles Farrell created photographs that aptly illustrated her text and made the protagonists approachable and recognizable. He made images that replicated what farm life was like, interpreting Sharpe's words into a believable world.

# Reflections

## Memory, Representation, and Change

KYRA A. KIETRYS, PH.D. | DAVIDSON COLLEGE

A s a professor of contemporary Spanish literature at Davidson College, I have extensive experience guiding conversations about verbal and visual texts. I expected the conversation about *Tobe* to proceed in a way I am used to: a conversation would develop organically from a list of prepared discussion questions. Yet, it was a completely different experience. Maybe because I am used to leading students through a discussion around texts that, at first glance, have seemingly little to do with them? (None of my students have direct or even indirect experience with the Spanish Civil War, 1936–39). In contrast, *Tobe*, while also from the 1930s, immediately hit a nerve. Each of us had thought deeply about our own experiences with race and representation, as well as how we saw race and representation depicted in *Tobe*. Our conversation was so spirited that I grew anxious about not addressing the brilliant questions crafted by Dr. Ashli Stokes and her team. Our rich discussion was spawned by each participant's passion, energy, and thoughtfulness but, how was I going to write about our conversation and organize my summary around the three required sections—text to self, text to text, text to world—if we were not more methodical in our dialogue? After reading through my notes and listening to the transcripts of our conversation, I realized that we had, in fact, spontaneously touched on more of the questions than I was able to systematically keep track of during our vibrant conversation.

As might be expected, each of our interpretations was shaped by our personal identities and past experiences. Thus arose a new challenge for me: Would I relay to you, the readers of this volume, the same information regarding the personal backgrounds that each participant shared during our conversation? Would I share their race and gender? Or, would I present a summary detached from these contexts? I decided that, in a volume about race, it did not make sense to pretend to be colorblind. I believe it is my ethical responsibility to share with you the same information I had that evening so you can interpret our conversation for yourselves. To do otherwise would be to pretend that we live in a postracial society. With that said, our group was comprised of one white male, one African American male, one African American female, two white females, and two white female students with audio recorders who did not participate in the conversation. The participants' ages ranged from the twenties through the sixties.

## Text to Self

All of us were able to relate to some aspect of Tobe's story. Each of us either came from a family of farmers, was African American, grew up in a predigital world, or all three. David Sanders, a member of Grier Heights Presbyterian Church, an African American male who grew up in North Carolina in the 1950s, was the participant who most directly identified with Tobe. He found many commonalities between his childhood and Tobe's. Micah Cash (The Light Factory), a white male and great-grandson of immigrants and farmers, identified with the agrarian lifestyle and believed that the loss of that world is what might make this book less accessible to today's readers. For me—a white female and great-granddaughter of immigrants who became farmers and miners—the representation of farm life was troubling because I perceived it as romanticized. For the most part, the book portrayed the children having a lot of fun, yet I knew from growing up as the granddaughter of farmers that farming was a tough life. We began to discuss whether or not *Tobe* accurately portrayed the reality of the son of African American tenant farmers in 1930s North Carolina. We did not come up with a single or simple answer. In some regards, some of us believed it did. For example, David and Mary Lou, a white couple from the South, identified with the concept of having to play outside all day as children. They had to find ways to invent their own fun while they stayed outside until dinnertime. We lamented that today is a different world in terms of safety, overscheduled children, and the phenomenon of screen time.

Tobe's anecdotes of the sweet potatoes, cotton, tobacco, and molasses all rang true to David. However, there was a problem with the peanuts. The book says, "We picked them off the vines" (p. 78). David remarked that anyone who has ever harvested peanuts knows they grow in the ground and not on vines; peanuts are not picked, they are dug up. We considered this error as

Taking notes during the conversations.

an example of where the voice of the white author was apparent. Clearly, she had never harvested peanuts. We began to talk about representation, voice-lessness, and tokenization. In addition to this demonstrably incorrect detail, was the questionable authenticity of the mother's speech. We agreed that a black woman farmer was not likely to say to her children, "Boys, I want you to pick some tomatoes for me to can. We shall need many cans of tomatoes this winter" (p. 112); but rather something like, "Baby, this is what we have to do to survive." Another participant at our table, Jessica Moss, the creative director at the Harvey B. Gantt Center, said she thinks a lot about voice and representation as a young artist and African American woman. She wondered if it was better to have this less-than-authentic and sometimes romanticized representation of blackness, or no representation of blackness at all? Some of us thought we should appreciate the efforts of Stella Gentry Sharpe who, as an educated white woman, was writing from a place of privilege. A black woman at the time would not have been able to publish Tobe's story. Moreover, Gentry Sharpe could not truly represent the complexities of the black world because she was not *of* that world. She could only represent what she observed of the black world and tell *their* story using *her* language and framework. *Tobe* is *her* story about *him*, it is not him speaking with agency. That said, the issue is more complicated than Tobe's mother simply speaking like a white mother. David reminded us that we should keep in mind that, at least in his experience in the South, black people lived in two worlds: "the public world and 'our' world." Perhaps Gentry Sharpe did not portray the difficult times in the way that Tobe's family lived them because they kept that part of their world private and out of Gentry Sharpe's view.

## Text to Text

Issues of representation in *Tobe* surfaced again in our conversation and became the segue into a discussion about other texts that represent African Americans. We discussed how American popular culture has evolved from the offensive, stereotypical, and boorish portrayal of African Americans in *Amos 'n' Andy* (1928–1960), whose original radio program was written by white authors and voiced by white actors. This program was denounced by some chapters of the NAACP as early as the 1930s (Barlow, 1999, p. 43). Incorporating black actors into *Amos 'n' Andy* when it became a television series did not make the program any less racist. In contrast, we now have programs like *black-ish* (2014–present), which has received multiple NAACP Image Awards (Bacle, 2017). The stories on *black-ish* are told by the people who are represented—they have their own voice (and voices, literally). The program is written and directed by African Americans, and its characters are college-educated, upper-middle-class families. The program is popularly touted as one that addresses racism across the diverse range of African Americans (Cheney, 2017). We asked ourselves if we would have gotten to programs like *black-ish* if it had not been for the first steps taken by efforts such as those of Gentry Sharpe. We also agreed that the television program *Empire* (2015–present) is a "super-high-octane ridiculous" representation, and *Scandal* (2012–present) is "a mess." These programs are simply spectacles, meaning that they give the general public something to gawk at but do not add any social value by working against racism.

Moss mentioned the importance of role models in her own childhood. She said Whitley on *A Different World* was the first time she saw someone who looked like her on television "who went to college and was sassy and cute." Whitley allowed her to consider the possibility that she, too, could go to college.

The concept of a lack of role models served as a transition in our conversation from contemporary television to earlier children's books and the availability of these books. We found that there are children's books with black protagonists—not always so easy to find, but they are there. David said he and his wife had boxes and boxes of children's books that they were giving to their adult children for their children. He fondly remembered *Whistle for Willie* (1964) by Ezra Jack Keats. Keats, a white man, is said to have broken "the color barrier in children's literature with the mainstream success of *The Snowy Day*, in 1962. He believed that all children should be able to see themselves in books they love" (Ezra Jack Keats Foundation, 2017, para. 5).

We saw that progress regarding representations of race in American popular culture is not linear. With that, our conversation evolved to a discussion about text to world.

## Text to World

We recognized that society today is fraught with issues of representation and authorship, particularly when black bodies and objectification are involved. In today's world, it is troubling when a white woman tells a black boy's experience. We found evidence in *Tobe*—such as the peanuts and the diction—to suggest that the author may not have based her story on a conversation with Tobe or his family, rather she framed her observations of them as their story. We asked, how can she claim that Tobe's story is *his* story if he did not have the opportunity to speak for himself, or have a voice in how he wanted his story to be told?

Two other issues made the power dynamic even more problematic for us: we learned in Benjamin Filene's opening remarks that Gentry Sharpe owned the land Tobe's family worked; and, it was unclear if she made money on the book, but it was likely that Tobe's family did not. We knew that the Garner family, who had posed as Tobe's family in the photographs, was not paid for their work as models (Watkins, 2015). While capitalizing on black bodies and black stories is a far cry from the brutality of slavery, it does seem to be an enduring legacy of slavery. Voice, authorship, and black bodies coalesced at this point in our conversation. Moss made some powerful points when she said:

> Learning today, though, that she *owned* the land . . . that little nugget of information, that caveat changes the entire story as well because then you think about [it]. I'm thinking about black business. I'm thinking about this family as becoming sustainable so that they can make money for themselves

using this farm. But she's benefitting from writing this text *about* them and describing them in the way she wants them to be seen, rather than (and this is debatable, because also I'm speaking about Tobe as if I know him and that relationship, and I don't) but, because she's created this framework now which is a text which is written and we're still reading it today. This is power. And, this is ownership. And, there's no . . . oh, let's have long conversations about objectifications of black bodies. Let's do it!

Jessica's interpretation was the closest our table came to discussing Black Lives Matter, which we never explicitly named.

From here we recognized that issues of agency and objectification were different in the 1930s than they are now. Some participants made the argument that we might consider a positive outcome of Tobe's objectification: Gentry Sharpe used her position of power and privilege to give voice to a constituency that had none. Moss noted that, "If she hadn't written this, there would be no representation of black families in agriculture, and then what?" And, today, while there may be fewer books about African American children than there are about white children, it is still more possible to write such a book than it was in the 1930s. Progress. But. Is it enough?

We moved to a conversation about our own experiences with diversity. David shared that when he worked for the city of Charlotte in the early nineties, his charge was to hire women and minorities to serve as firefighters. Charlotte was the first city to include women firefighters. Cash's sixteen-month-old son, who is white and attends a racially diverse day care, recognizes different races and identifies easily with black children because he spends his days in a racially diverse setting. Moss was curious as to how Cash knew that his son was aware of different races. Cash replied that his son "lights up when he sees another black child in public," attributing this positive affective reaction to his son's experience in daycare. While Cash added the caveat that he is not a social scientist, there is, in fact, empirical evidence demonstrating that infants as young as three months old are able to distinguish between races (Sangrioli and De Schonen, 2004). Our table agreed that it would be encouraging if all of society could have this same positive interracial experience.

We asked ourselves, what about Tobe's story makes him black? If it were not for the pictures, which reveal the color of skin, would we have known that he was black? Some participants thought his name was a hint—he must be black because he had an original name. Other than that, it was the photographs—not the text—that revealed Tobe's race. David's wish for his own children was for them to learn from a young age that "being African American means something different than just the color of their skin." Would today's reader learn this lesson from *Tobe*?

## References

Anonymous. (2017). Ezra Jack Keats Foundation. Retrieved from http://www.ezra-jack-keats.org/.

Bacle, Ariana. (2017). "*Black-ish* Wins Big at NAACP Image Awards." *Entertainment Weekly*. February 12. Retrieved from http://ew.com/tv/2017/02/12/naacp-image-awards-2017-blackish/.

Barlow, William. (1999). *Voice Over: The Making of Black Radio*. Philadelphia: Temple University Press.

Cheney, Jen. (2017). "In Praise of *Black-ish*'s Extraordinary Election Episode." *Vulture, Devouring Culture*. January 11. Retrieved from http://www.vulture.com/2017/01/blackish-election-episode-captures-the-mood-in-america.html

Sangrigoli, Sandy, and De Schonen, Scania. (2004). "Recognition of Own-Race and Other-Race Faces by Three-Month-Old Infants." *Journal of Child Psychology and Psychiatry*, 45(7), 1219–1227.

Watkins, Charles. (2015). Comment on John Blythe's "The Story Behind the Children's Book *Tobe*" in *North Carolina Miscellany: Exploring the History, Literature, and Culture of the Tar Heel State*. Retrieved from http://blogs.lib.unc.edu/ncm/index.php/2012/10/24/the-story-behind-the-childrens-book-tobe/.

# Tobe

Race, Representation, Identity, and a Need "To Be"

DEBRA C. SMITH, PH.D. | UNC CHARLOTTE

S tella Gentry Sharpe displayed commitment to fulfilling a young boy's dream of seeing himself in books, while simultaneously exposing conflict that can occur in the intersection of race, representation, and identity. What seemed a simple gesture to create inclusive literature at a little boy's request, reveals the tendency of an author to tell a story from her own place of knowledge, experience, and even privilege. While the book and story of Tobe is a valiant effort by an empathetic author, in some ways it can be examined as an exercise in *impostorism* as well as an application of dual identity. With regard to impostorism, Tobe is presented through the lens of the author and is, in fact, almost a fraud in the book. Tobe is the son of a sharecropper. Sharecroppers often were indebted to and exploited by landowners, such that they remained stagnant economically. In the book, readers needed to suspend disbelief and eschew history in order to relate to the stories about Tobe, his lifestyle, and his family, as sharecropping was never mentioned. The first story "Tobe and His Brothers" is actually an exercise in futility as the reader is challenged by the question "can you find Tobe?" while presented with a picture of a group of black boys. In actuality, there is no true picture of Tobe, either among the group of boys or in the book at all. Even the photograph captioned to be Tobe in the book is revealed to not be a photograph of him at all. Our group explored these themes of impostorism and inclusivity throughout our discussion.

## Text to Self: Could we relate to Tobe's Story?

The author's ability to create a dual identity for Tobe, though there is no picture of him in the book, is evident. Tobe wanted to see children who looked like him in books—children with black skin and kinky hair. Sharpe develops

Ellanor Graves considers the depictions of African American farm life of the era.

Tobe's story in such a way that his racial identity complements the identity she has crafted for him. She does this by highlighting cultural experiences and ideology that resonated with readers, especially those who shared Tobe's racial identity. A black family in the 1930s considered basic universal luxuries of food, shelter, and family to be their main sources of wealth. Our group talked about how small pleasures like sewing clothes, helping in the kitchen, picking wild fruit from trees, and spending time with family were the foundations for survival among southern African American families.

For a child to feel noticed is essential to their own identity development. Thus, even in its simplicity, there is some credibility and authenticity indicative of the dual identity that the author created for Tobe. For example, stories that appealed to the African American readers' senses and experiences like picking blackberries and peaches, making molasses, and ice cream, were relatable. Despite the lack of context, we could fill in the gaps based upon our own experience. Further, life in rural North Carolina in the 1930s did indeed include picking cotton, setting rabbit traps, pulling and curing tobacco, and storing tomatoes for the winter. The appeal of the dual identity of Tobe is that, while the book seemed sanitized and exclusive of the real-life experiences of growing up black in the South, it served the purpose of demonstrating the innovation of

A group working through the issues of expressing of *Tobe*'s voice.

children to create adventure and fun within their circumstances as they played barefoot on a farm. Free of the twenty-first century technology that occupy children today, the book explored themes of curiosity, family, sharing, nature, hard work, gratitude, peace, and joy as they went about the business of life. In developing Tobe's dual identity, Sharpe captured tenets of African American culture by showing children filing into church, which historically has served the purpose of schooling black children, emphasizing values, and providing extended family.

Our discussion group's first impressions of Tobe emphasized Sharpe's impostorism in that that there appeared to be a disconnect between the book's photographs and the text, especially if the full reality of life in the 1930s for African Americans was taken into account. The book lacked the complexity inherent in rural life in North Carolina, and instead posited a happy-go-lucky life free of racial conflict, struggle, and hardship. The book was simplistic and revealed the author's ignorance about the nature of conversation among black families, instead relying on contrived and inauthentic dialogue. Some members of our reading group argued that Sharpe succeeded as an ethnographer in listening to Tobe, envisioning his environment through her own lens, and relaying his voice in some way. On the other hand, she was less successful in this regard as she was attempting to envision how she believed a conversation would be and what a story would be, all from her own perspective, and clearly in her own voice.

### Text to Text: Romanticizing Southern African American Life

Certainly, Sharpe romanticized Tobe's story, almost in *Dick and Jane* elemental story fashion. The stories abandoned any references to conflict. Yet, conflict, journey, and place are all themes inherent in African American literature and serve as a foundation for story. As an outsider to African American culture, Sharpe neglects that African American literature examines the role of African Americans within the larger context of American society—conflict and all—in favor of presenting a fantastical representation of life for a sharecropper's son. This technique by Sharpe reminded one of our reading group members of her attempt to collect her Latina grandmother's life story. When she enlisted her mother to assist with transcribing her notes, her mother sanitized the original script of its slang, regionalism, and realness. Though innocent in her attempts to edit, her mother replicated what Sharpe did in telling Tobe's story. Thus, the book *Tobe* cannot be fully and entirely appreciated as a historical piece as it does not represent the experience of African American sharecroppers more holistically.

Further, it was apparent that some of the pictures were staged as cameras and picture-taking were not as readily accessible in the 1930s as they are now. Staged pictures often led our reading group to lament that the innocence in something as simple as children getting dirty from planting flowers and taking care of a garden was stripped away by an accompanying picture that presented pristine little girls in flowered dresses. Our reading group noticed that one of the most authentic pictures in *Tobe* was of their school, a Rosenwald School. Rosenwald Schools were born of the collaboration between Booker T. Washington and the philanthropist Julius *Rosenwald*, to build schools for African American children in the South.

### Text to World: What *Tobe* Helps to Portray about African American Life

The theme of family is explored in a more representative way through *Tobe*'s introduction of grandmother's calf, planning for Thanksgiving dinner, and the close relationship Tobe shares with his siblings and cousins. Tobe's big brother Raeford helps his mother with Thanksgiving dinner by gathering pears and apples while the twins get hickory nuts and their father brings rabbits. Tobe's mother bakes chickens and her daughters bake cakes and sweet potato pies. This type of collaboration by black families is often marginalized in favor of presenting dysfunction. Yet, stories of family strength and harmony are not anomalies. One of our reading group members recalled Sunday afternoons in the winter in the 1930s as she sat on her mother's lap as her mother read to her. Similarly, in the story "Peanuts," in first-person voice Tobe says that when he and his siblings were "full of peanuts and stories, we go to bed" (p. 78).

The strength of the book lies in its ability to focus on simplicity in contrast to the age in which we now live, its ability to represent African American family, culture and, values in a way that had often been misrepresented, stereotyped, or erased from media altogether. Lessons were taught when Tobe's mother told Big Boy that "there's no such thing as luck" (p. 117), when Tobe's mother gave him a tin box with pepper in it to retaliate against a bully, or when Tobe did not get a nickel from his Aunt Mary because he did not complete his chore. The parents in Tobe took time to explain and impart education into their children ("Daddy plants cotton to buy clothes for you to wear to school" (p 58), while demonstrating the results of hard work. Our reading group said that work seemed like fun—from making a rabbit trap, to picking cotton, to harvesting sweet potatoes, but also taught that hard work yielded results. Tobe said, "when we get big like Daddy, we can (cure tobacco) too" (p. 53). While our reading group was critical of the author's lack of depth in these representations of family and values, they were relatable and accurate in a way that others stories and pictures in the book were not.

It is rare to see a picturesque illustration of black life in American media even if it exists. Media representations often depict African American families as fragmented, suffering economic inequality, female-headed, and crime-ridden among other characteristics. Tobe represents what a lot of African American children experienced. They might have grown up poor but were not aware that they were poor. They were rich in family, religion, lessons learned, sharing, and happy experiences. Sharpe's dual identity for Tobe acknowledged this wealth even as she imposed upon us a young, black, son of a sharecropper, whose idyllic existence within the pages of a book compelled readers to suspend disbelief while granting his wish "to be."

# Tobe, Dick and Jane

Rereading the American Primer

CHERYL BUTLER-BRAYBOY, PH.D | JOHNSON C. SMITH
UNIVERSITY

On Wednesday, April 26, 2017, a diverse group of North Carolina residents and readers gathered to discuss *Tobe* in collective conversation. The participants were divided into round tables of seven to eight persons each, including one moderator. It was the moderator's job to introduce topics of conversation and to synthesize and contextualize thematic threads. I served as moderator of Table 7; there were nine tables in all. Our members included Eleanor Graves of Ben Salem Presbyterian Church, Stephanie Misko of the Vanguard Group, Barbara Simpson of the Grier Heights Community, Kristine Slade and Debra Smith of UNC Charlotte, Banu Valladares of the North Carolina Humanities Council, and myself, an associate professor of English at Johnson C. Smith University. Here are my observations about the discussion.

In 1939, black folks in the Deep South were embroiled in a daily battle, fighting mightily against discriminatory Jim Crow laws, de facto segregation, acts of intimidation, and violence. This is a dark chapter in American history, universally known, rendered permanent through newspaper clippings, legal briefs, autobiographical accounts, grotesque art, and gut-wrenching photographs. Black authors—Claude McKay, W. E. B. DuBois, Richard Right, Zora Neale Hurston, Jean Toomer, and others—documented the period in bold, textured tones to describe the pain and humiliation of daily life. They used a complex language and reverberating tropes like the mask and the veil, the photo and the mirror, to represent the duality of the black experience: to be black (oppressed) and American (equal) without contradiction. This is not the case in the book *Tobe*, written by Stella Gentry Sharpe, published—for

Cheryl Butler-Brayboy discusses her group's findings with the larger gathering.

the first time—by the UNC Press in 1939. Gentry Sharpe was a white woman who had worked as a teacher in North Carolina. She tells the story of a young black boy, her neighbor Tobe, and his family in the throes of country life in rural North Carolina. Gentry Sharpe asserts Tobe as the first-person narrator, a six-year-old black boy, anxious to tell his story. The book is a gift to the young boy who complained to Gentry Sharpe that he could not see himself in schoolbooks. He expressed a sentiment once expressed by a young Zora Neale Hurston: "Where's me. I can't see me" (Hurston, 1928). In her book, *Tobe*, Gentry Sharpe made black "recognition"—rather than "misrecognition"—possible.

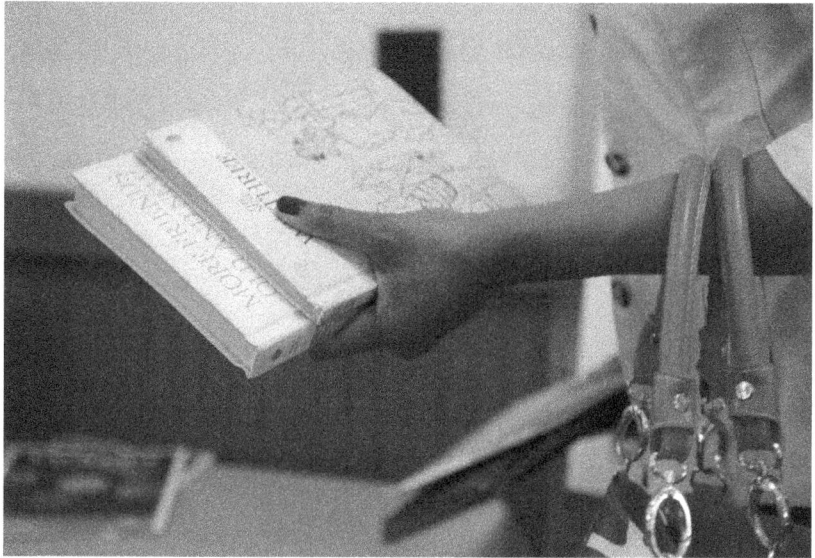

A participant brings examples of African American depictions of the time period.

## Text to Self

*Recognition* is the experience of seeing "self" reflected in dominant representations of social life. It is literally the experience, for African American social subjects in this case, of seeing "self" depicted accurately in books, magazines, newspapers, and photographs with his/her full humanity—intelligence, innocence and all—on display in full sight. Seeing "self" in books, newspapers, and magazines was, in the early twentieth century, a double-edged experience. In one sense, real life was crazier than fiction. Real-life depictions of African Americans documented real-life horrors: lynchings, cross burnings, mob threats, and more. In another sense, representations of "blackness" were grotesquely stereotypical: Uncle Tom, Huck Finn's Jim, Sambo—not to mention blackface minstrelsy of the day. As you can imagine, *mis-recognition,* the experience of altering the depicted image to a more acceptable image in one's mind was a strategy of psychological survival. According to the *Oxford Reference* (2017), *misrecognition* is the "process of self-identification in which a subject assumes an identity they mistake for their own" (para. 1). The theory emerges from Jacques Derrida's work on the mirroring phase of childhood development. The subject's "'I' is the product of its imaginary and the result of an illusion" (*Oxford Reference*, 2017, para. 1). In the case of the earlier twentieth century African American young reader, like *Tobe,* seeing was not believing. Based on his statement to Gentry Sharpe, Tobe was the quintessential "resisting spectator" who used active reading techniques to reject exclusionary images of dominant American life—*Dick and Jane* among them, perhaps—that could *not* reflect his story. Tobe did not *misrecognize* stories like *Dick and Jane,* tinting the characters' white skin with brown tones in his head. Instead, Tobe absorbed the characters on face value and rejected the stories they told. His inquiry to Gentry Sharpe was a radical act of courage. Tobe requested accurate self-representation as an act of self-reclamation. Gentry Sharpe took a bold step of her own: to right a racial wrong, to document, in realistic tones, the story of black boys like Tobe, and to allow his voice to sound as the self-celebrating narrator with powers of literacy, critical thinking, and keen self-awareness. Was Tobe's request fulfilled? Is the portrayal realistic and accurate?

*Tobe* documents a slice of life: rural black sharecroppers, Tobe, and his family, who live and love in the South. The pictures reflect a family's jubilation amid mundane and otherwise perfunctory acts: caring for the hens, pigs, goats and cows, wading in the water, picking cotton, riding in a tire, picking blueberries, making ice cream, turning the grindstone, and more. Tobe is the hero of the story, a young black boy who is precocious, wise beyond his years, articulate, and thoughtful. As primary narrator of this alleged memoir, he introduces the reader to his family and shares the events that unfold in the course of a summer in their rural North Carolina neighborhood. The language is simplistic and clear. The photos reflect realism with an uncanny spin toward optimism.

Our group—all women—had a vibrant conversation—not a debate, about *Tobe*. Each idea articulated by a participant would engender rich reflection on the part of other participants and the pondering of points of intersection: where our lives conjoined with Tobe's life as documented in vibrant black and white. Banu, for example, could relate to the innocent country life reminiscent of her grandmother's childhood in Venezuela, but she did not embrace the book's primer-like approach to African American autobiography. Barbara found the book a celebration of rural North Carolina family life. Like Tobe, she recalled the thrill of running through the tall grass with summer-singed bare feet, and the refreshment of a spontaneous toe dip in the creek. For Barbara, the book was an authentic depiction of her life. Reading *Tobe* was a trip down memory lane.

Participants agreed: the language in *Tobe* is simple but the images—in the second half of the book—are vibrant. Both the pictures and words offer a brand of imagery that acutely enlivens the senses of taste, touch, sight, sound, and smell. Still, some participants argued that there was a disconnect between the verbal narrative and the photographic tale being told. The group seemed to prefer the complexity of the visual storytelling enacted by photographer Charles Farrell.

Interesting enough, it was the written narrative that triggered the most impassioned discussion. The prevailing question centered around the authenticity of narrative voice. Was Tobe speaking his truth through this book, or was the author, Stella Gentry Sharpe appropriating Tobe's story and asserting her own voice, one that offered a filtered interpretation of Tobe's black rural experience. This was a necessary topic of discussion. Here is how the discussion unfolded.

Barbara's story struck a chord with every woman in the group. She was born in 1939, the year *Tobe* was published. Reading was an essential part of her childhood, and she would have been thrilled to have read a story like *Tobe* back then. Barbara connected with the stories of adventure and innocence. Many of the adventures described by Tobe, were adventures she had experienced in her childhood. She and her cousins had the same innate curiosity. Like Tobe, Barbara liked going in the woods and finding snakes, wading in the creek, and more. She indicated the absence of white/black racial conflict in the book was not alarming or unusual. She says white and black children during her childhood climbed trees together, rode bikes together, and even spent the night at one another's homes. She says the colorblind aspect of the book was real and authentically represents the experience of country life in the era. Indeed, Barbara "recognized" herself in the face of Tobe.

Banu, too, experienced some moments of recognition. She saw a disconnect between the photos and the words in the book. She wanted to see more personal stories in the book. In addition, she noticed a narrative shift between the primer—*Dick and Jane*—writing style in the beginning of the book to the more complex personal stories articulated toward the end of the book. She thought the editor might have identified the shift in voice and substance and requested revision. To her, when the personal stories are introduced, the book comes alive! These stories about Tobe and his siblings riding in a tire and more, reminded her of stories shared by her grandmother, stories of a joyful childhood in Venezuela.

Similar to Banu's experience, Debra enjoyed the stories depicted in the second half of the book, stories about blackberry picking, peach canning, and more. She initially believed—like most of us—that Tobe and his family were the actual people depicted in the photographs that accompany the story. When she learned that the people photographed were actors posing as Tobe and his family for the book, she felt a sense of detatchment from the story. Still, Smith finds the beauty of the book in its ability to trigger connection in readers. She found herself stepping into the text and filling in gaps with her own stories of blueberry picking and more. In a sense, Smith used strategies of misrecognition to employ imagination in places where the narrative fell short.

Ellanor also recognized the limitations in the text and was frustrated by the simplicity of the language Gentry Sharpe used to represent Tobe's experience. She felt the language was inauthentic and contrived. Still, she appreciates Gentry Sharpe's initiative, the desire to help an African American child see "self" in a book. She wished Gentry Sharpe had offered more complexity of thought and language, an authentic language Tobe and his family members likely expressed. In contrast, Eleanor was impressed by elements of adventure that were adequately represented in the text: black berry picking, pulling tobacco, building a see-saw, and rolling around in an old tire. *Tobe* and his siblings saw a challenge and fought to overcome it. If there was conflict, they worked it out in a harmonious way. These were moments of "recognition" for Eleanor.

Stephanie was impressed by the respect Tobe and his siblings displayed toward their parents. She also was struck by the children's work effort; Tobe and his siblings saw work as fun. Like Banu, Debra, and Eleanor, she enjoyed the stories told in the second half of the book, like the story about luck. Mama says there is no such thing as luck. The moral of the story: work brings good luck. Stephanie noticed that this text focuses on the simple aspects of life and diverges from the themes and writing approaches generally found in African American literature. Stephanie did not employ "misrecognition" to ensure Tobe matched the discourses of traditional African American literature.

Robin offered a realistic interpretation, as well. She acknowledged that most of us expect Tobe, naturally, to document the stories of real people with textured lives. Like most in the group, Robin initially felt alienated from the tone of the text. Nevertheless, Robin indicated that children's stories are—by genre—distilled stories. Robin grew up reading *Dick and Jane. Dick and Jane* stories, like *Tobe,* are distilled, contrived stories. Robin found the subject of "representation" perhaps more revealing than the subject of voice. As the discussion unfolded, Robin's perspective evolved. Like Eleanor, Robin began to see a complexity in Gentry Sharpe's initiative, the idea of launching the ambitious book venture in response to a child's desire to see "self" in a book. Perhaps this was the only way Gentry Sharpe could give Tobe voice. Robin indicated how important it is to give a child a sense they are noticed—and have place in the world. Gentry Sharpe's mission was a noble one, in this respect.

## Text to Text: Children's Books of the Era

Most at Table 7 agreed: *Tobe* absorbs the currency of the *Dick and Jane* series. They hit the scholastic market in the 1930s, and were an immediate hit. According to expert Mark Mancini, *Dick and Jane* series creator, Zerna Sharp thought she could create a series of books that students would devour. The appeal: simple words, educational content, simple plot, entertaining topics, relatable characters, and vibrant illustrations to bring the stories to life. Sharp brought the idea to education scholar, William Gray, who saw the immediate merit of the idea. Sharp is a former teacher who understands the strengths and deficiencies of young American readers. Much like *Tobe's* writer, Stella Gentry Sharpe, the teacher was inspired by the uninspired student, the one who felt locked out of academic culture, the one who needed to "see me" in the stories of the day, the one who craved *recognition*. In each case—the case of Sharp and Gentry Sharpe—the creation of a book was philanthropic work, indeed (Mancini, 2015).

   Even philanthropic educational endeavors come with their flaws. Years after the publishing and consumption bonanza of the *Dick and Jane* books, the series faced harsh criticism for being misogynistic, racially exclusionary, and hegemonic. Still, you can't diminish the numbers. Between 1930 and 1970, eighty-five million first graders had read *Dick and Jane* books as part of their formal education. *Tobe*, in contrast, was read by a targeted and minimal audience in North Carolina schools and the book never made its way to national prominence like the *Dick and Jane* series, but the narrative styles are strikingly similar. This makes some critical readers think *Tobe's* author, Gentry Sharpe, aimed to create a "black" *Dick and Jane* book that would serve as a primer for a more diverse American audience. Some see Gentry Sharpe's aim as noble. Others, in contrast, question the "authenticity" of *Tobe's* first-person narrative voice. Is *Tobe* an authentic black memoir or is it an inauthentic text through which Gentry Sharpe ventriloquizes the voice of *Tobe* through a mainstream white narrator who replicates the story of Dick and Jane in blackface? Is the narrative original and revolutionary or a simple act of literary mimicry?

Furthermore, the *Dick and Jane* series bolstered the "look and say" approach to literacy. Children learned to associate the visual portrayal of Dick and Jane with the words printed on the page (Mancini, 2015). Gentry Sharpe seems to execute the similar look and say approach. As young readers plowed through words on the page, their eyes grazed the beautifully captured photographs of Tobe's "family" on the adjacent pages. In some cases, the pictures tell a more complex story of black survival and black cultural abundance than the simple words can convey.

Based on the discussion at Table 7 surrounding the pictures and words in *Tobe*, it became clear: *Tobe* offers few clues about whose words are depicted on the page. For example, African American slave narratives of the nineteenth century often tackled the dilemma of narrative authenticity head on in the preface and editorial notes. Harriett Jacobs, author of *Incidents in the Life of a Slave Girl,* asserted in the preface of her book that she wrote the book herself, to make the story appropriate for white women readers of the North. She writes: "Reader be assured this narrative is no fiction. I am aware that some of my adventures may seem incredible; but they are, nevertheless, strictly true. I have not exaggerated the wrongs inflicted by Slavery; in the contrary, my descriptions fall far short of the facts" (Jacobs, 1861). Jacobs's editor, Lydia Maria Child, a white patron, also included a defense of the author in her "Introduction by the Editor." Child acknowledges that she "pruned excrescences" from the book, but she did not alter the language of the slave author:

> At her request, I have revised her manuscript; but such changes as I have made have been mainly for purposes of condensation and orderly arrangement. I have not added anything to the incidents, or changed the import of her very pertinent remarks. With trifling exceptions, both the ideas and the language are her own. (Jacobs, 1861, p. 10)

These words by the slave author and white woman patron confirm that the formal slave, Harriett Jacobs—a black woman born in 1815—had written the book herself. The authenticating prefatory documents were rudimentary and compulsory in published slave narratives of the eighteenth and nineteenth centuries. Historically, black-white literary collaborations—in the antebellum and Jim Crow periods—demanded statements of authenticity. Resisting white audiences might otherwise doubt the intellectual capacity and narrative the veracity of documented experiences of authors of color offering complexity of thought in bold and unforgiving print. Literacy itself—of black authors—would otherwise be questioned. Gentry Sharpe's text is missing these authenticating documents, an omission that triggers doubt and skepticism in modern-day audiences.

Gentry Sharpe offers an "Acknowledgments," in which she thanks a list of colleagues in academia and publishing:

> I am especially indebted to Dr. M. R. Trabue, formerly head of the Department of Education in the University of North Carolina, now Dean of the School of Education in Pennsylvania State College, for encouragement in the writing of *Tobe;* to Miss Nora Beust, of the School of Library Science in the University of North Carolina; to Dr. Guy B. Johnson and Dr. L. M. Brooks, of the Department of Sociology in the University of North Carolina, for reading the manuscript and making many helpful suggestions; to Mr.s Alice T. Paine, of the University of North Carolina Press, for her editing of the manuscript; and to Mr. Charles Farrell, whose photographs have caught the spirit of the text so completely and have made possible the carrying out of a long delayed plan. (Gentry Sharpe, 1939, p. x)

Perhaps most striking here is what Gentry Sharpe omits: a message of gratitude to Tobe and his family, discussions of authenticity. What was her role as ethnographer, writer, and storyteller? How did Tobe "dictate" the stories to her? Did she "edit" Tobe's words, and if so, why, and to what extent? The absence of answers leaves much room for speculation.

## Close Readings

The narrative begins with an introduction of Tobe, written in the third person:

> This is Tobe and his brothers.
> They live on a farm.
> They have many pets.
> Tobe is not a big boy.
> He has no twin.
> Can you find him?

The accompanying photograph features a wagon carrying five smiling black boys with bare feet and collared shirts. There is an older boy leaning over a large wheel of the wagon; he wears long pants and a big grin. The boys may range in age from four to ten years old. They seem happy and relaxed, enjoying a typical day on the farm. Strangely, the introduction/exposition of the book seems to be told from the perspective of the author, Stella Gentry Sharpe. All subsequent pages—121 pages total—are told in the first person, Tobe rises up as the narrator. For example, on page 2 of the book, Tobe introduces himself:

I am Tobe.
My real name is Clay Junior.
Tobe is a nickname.
I am six years old.
I go to school.
We have fun on our farm.
I will tell you about it.

The simple sentences mimic the sound and style often assumed by a six-year-old storyteller. The voice sounds authentic. Still the abrupt shift from third-person narrator to first-person narrator is jarring and comes without explanation. The photograph that accompanies the narrative here is a tight shot of "Tobe"—although we later learned that the people in the photos are actors who stage the stories told by the real-life Tobe. Tobe is wearing a crisp pair of overalls and a collared shirt. He is smiling and pointing his finger toward someone off screen, perhaps the photographer. He is sitting on a bench, savoring the summer sun.

As the narrative progresses, the story moves beyond biographical introductions of Tobe, his brothers, sisters, and parents, to an adventure story. On page 14, *Tobe* tells the story of "Tom, Our Pet Cat:"

This is our pet cat. His name is Tom.
One day a big boy caught our cat
And put him in the brook.
We called our Mother.
She made the big boy go home.
We Feed our cat and play with him.
We do not hurt him.
He is not afraid of us.

The language is simple and honest, but there is a shift here. The narrator shares a specific memory. He discusses one day in the life, and the specific story of Tobe begins to channel the universal "childhood" experience of first pet ownership. This is a story of conflict and adventure, told in abbreviated and optimistic tones. The adjacent photograph depicts two young boys seated on a bench, dressed in overall shorts. One boy is leaning over, petting the cat. The other boy appears to be feeding the cat a snack (p. 14–15). These are experiences to which every reader—white, black, Latino, Asian—can connect.

Later in the text, on page 16, Tobe introduces the story called "Our School." He writes:

This is our school.
We keep it nice and clean.
We have trees in the yard.
We are planting some bushes.
When they grow, the yard will be pretty.

The adjacent photo depicts three teen girls standing and three teen boys sitting outside their schoolhouse. A few other students are scattered about the schoolyard. The girls are dressed fashionably in dresses, hair perfectly coiffed. The boys are dapper, wearing slacks and hats for the educational sojourn. There is no mention—in the narrative or in the posture of the photo—of Jim Crow, segregated schools, or unsavory threats. Life is good, free of trauma, free of race-based torment. This is the rarely told story of early twentieth century black life in America. Families did have meaningful home, church, and school experiences in spite of racial tensions of the day. Daily life for black folk often is devoid of violence and rich with cultural celebration, but much of this history gets overridden by the quantum racial experiences of conflict and experiences that often attract reporters and cameras. The mundane and frivolous black experiences of the good life get left out of public accounts. Table 7 concluded that *Tobe* offers a refreshing and unique glimpse into the real lives of rural blacks in the 1930s. There is life beyond racial strife, and Gentry Sharpe and Charles Farrell succeed in capturing the authenticity of this journey.

## Text to World

Finally, *Tobe* is a gift to twenty-first century readers. Perhaps it offers a constructed narrative voice that mimics the voice of Sharp's *Dick and Jane*. Still, the effect is powerful and the net end consequence of the narrative construction—a black-white collaboration—is an authentic representation of black rural life in the 1930s, a life that could and often did exist beyond the confines of race and racial conflict of the day. To survive in America, American (including African American) social subjects often have to remember this racial history and simultaneously forget it. They have to understand how the mistakes of an American past may shape the present vis-à-vis issues of education, poverty, and incarceration. At the same time, black social subjects must intermittently forget the painful history to live unhindered by the low expectations prescribed by American racial ideology that once established a hierarchy of races with whites at the top and blacks at the bottom. *Tobe*—Table 7 concluded—represents a goal achieved. Tobe and his family arrive to a twenty-first century readership as round characters who emerge as dignified, socially integrated, intelligent, and articulate societal players. Their lives were rich and their legacy is, too. The Gentry Sharpe/Farrell/*Tobe* collaboration offers a needed, authentic moment of reprieve from the American race fight. It is a moment of recognition to the previously excluded reader. It is a literary caesura where *Tobe* and *Dick and Jane* can coexist in harmony and without apology.

## References

Derrida, Jacques. (1998). *Of Grammatology.* Baltimore: Johns Hopkins University Press.

Hurston, Zora Neale. (1928, May). How It Feels to Be Colored Me. *World Tomorrow,* 11, 215–216.

Jacobs, Harriet. (1861; 2001). *Incidents in the Life of a Slave Girl.* Boston: Dover Publications.

Mancini, Mark. (2015). *Rare Book School: 15 Fun Facts about Dick and Jane.* http://www.mentalfloss.com.

Oxford Reference. (2017). http://www.oxfordreference.com.

Sharpe, Stella Gentry. (1939). *Tobe.* Chapel Hill: University of North Carolina Press.

# In Search of a Better Mirror

Race, Representation, and Identity

DEBORAH JUNG | WINDING SPRINGS ELEMENTARY

As an Asian American raised in the South during the 1960s, I saw my ancestry reflected, sometimes in brilliant cadmium yellow, in books like Thomas Handforth's *Mei Li*, Marjorie Flack's *Ping,* and Claire Bishop's *Five Chinese Brothers*. In my early teens, I joined the family restaurant business just after the end of the Vietnam War. During that period, I became very aware of both race and gender as social issues, not only in the news, but also in daily interactions with our customers. In my twenties and thirties, when I worked in the local public library, I saw and experienced less racial prejudice since I was working in a branch that served a socio-economically diverse area. I actually experienced more racial prejudice after I switched careers and joined the local school system, where race and ethnicity had for years been synonymous with economic status. For the past few years, I have been trying to add more authors and illustrators of color to the library collection to better reflect the ethnic diversity in the school in which I work. Both personally and professionally, the depiction of people of color in children's books is a concern of mine, so when I was invited to a book discussion of *Tobe* by Stella Gentry Sharpe, I jumped at the chance.

The table to which I was assigned was primarily Caucasian and primarily academics. In addition to the educators, we had one member of the local community, Mae Israel, as well as historian Benjamin Filene and a representative from the UNC Press. At first, we were all cautious, trying to be politically correct, but as the conversation became deeper, comments became more spontaneous and heartfelt.

In the end, there were three major questions that this group explored:

· Is this an authentic representation of black families in this time period?
· Did this book clear a path for the inclusion of African Americans in children's picture books?

· Since the creators were white, is this a positive portrayal of African Americans? Was it seen as a positive portrayal then? Is it one now?

## Text to Self: Is this an authentic representation of black families in this time period?

Although our first comments were about the text itself, the conversation quickly moved to our perceptions. The initial comments were that the book seemed to be an idyllic rosy picture of farm life that did not include the racial and social discrimination of the period. Mae, our community representative, made the comment that children are not necessarily privy to the worldly concerns of adults and the text reflects the concerns of children—pets, fun, family, and exploring their environment. While poverty was evident in the vehicles and buildings in the photographs, it was unclear from their staging whether this was meant to portray the black tenant farmer family as happy, hardworking, and stoic or whether the photographs were meant to perpetuate the pathological, happily submissive Uncle Tom stereotype. According to Rita Smith, quoting the dust jacket of *Tobe* in a 2005 transcript for *Recess!*, photographs were thought to be the best medium to record "the rich actualities of their lives and personalities" (Smith, 2005). While posed and a little contrived, the images were similar to Dorothea Lange's photos of both black and white tenant farmers in Person County during the summer of 1939. And the simple text did describe some of the realities of a hard life—the near constant work it took to raise sufficient food, the death of a family hen, and dealing with a local bully. It seemed to describe a life of simple pleasures. The photographs and the text seemed to resonate as being true to the subsistence level labor of tenant farms in the post-Depression period in the rural South as well as portraying commonly held stereotypes.

## Text to text: Did this book clear a path for the inclusion of African Americans in Children's picture books?

Ironically, we are still asking today the same question that Tobe asked Stella Gentry Sharpe eighty years ago. At the time of *Tobe's* publication, the two best-known picture books featuring "coloreds" would have been a variation of the fool folktale called *Epaminondas and His Auntie* and Helen Bannerman's *Story of Little Black Sambo*. Most likely, the people at our table speculated,

Examples of African American children's literature at the reception.

adult titles, such as *The Bible* or *The Green Book*, would be found in homes of this period. Other children's books of the era would have been what we now consider classic chapter books, such as *Gulliver's Travels* or *Andersen's Fairy Tales*, with few illustrations. Gentry Sharpe's wholesome depiction of an African American boy and his family would probably have been very welcome in black households. My own memories of popular children's books published in the thirties and forties were of blue-eyed, blonde, well-behaved children, and a quick perusal of internet resources, such as Goodreads.com and The Baldwin Library of Historical Children's Literature at the University of Florida, confirmed my memories. Throughout the last century there have been attempts to introduce juvenile books and magazines for a black audience, which by and large have not been successful. W. E. B DuBois published *The Brownies Book* as a positive magazine for African American children that featured stories as well as articles, and attempted to promote nonstereotypical images of blacks. That magazine lasted only two years. While black authors like Ellen Tarry did have children's books published, they seem to have disappeared into obscurity. The next notable children's book that I remember featuring nonstereotype African American characters did not arrive until about 1962, when Ezra Jack Keats's *Snowy Day* was published. *Snowy Day* went on to win the Caldecott Award the following year. Keats was not black and race was not mentioned in the text, but the beautiful artwork and universal appeal of the illustrations still attracts children to this day. Later, when questioned, Keats would say that blacks should have been in children's books all along; and indeed, long before ethnic diversity was popular, Keats's books showed children playing in what was clearly a diverse urban neighborhood. Most important for the purposes of this essay is that the Caldecott Award guaranteed that *Snowy Day* would remain in publication and on bookstore and library shelves for years—not only would it increase exposure of this book to many, many more people but also that generations of Americans would come to treasure it as an example of excellence in children's literature and share it with their own children. In the early 1970s, the Coretta Scott King Award began bringing notable and rising African American writers and artists to public attention, and because of the awards, these books became easier to market to mainstream customers. In recent years, a number of picture books won both Caldecott Honors and the Coretta Scott King Award. Still, black authors and illustrators are underrepresented in children's literature. Early readers that feature African Americans are even more rare.

One of the questions our table had was whether *Tobe* was used in schools. The text, simple sentences with short words at the beginning of the book, became longer and more complex. By the end of the book, a chapter would span two pages. We hypothesized that the book was designed to be used as a reading primer. According to Filene, there are letters in UNC's archives from teachers and parents thanking the author for writing the book. So this book was probably used by both for teaching students to read. Since the book ends abruptly, we then asked one another if there was more information about Tobe and his family. Some of this was answered during the lecture at the beginning of the book talk, including about how the Garner family posed for the photographs. More questions were answered at the table by Filene, including information about the lawsuit that Charles Garner's father wanted to institute against Farrell. I located a reference to this lawsuit at Wilson Library at UNC Chapel Hill in Charles Farrell's papers, but I did not locate any legal documents among the papers. I did not have time to go through them all, so perhaps there are more references to be found in that file box. More interesting for me as a librarian, catalog entries at Wilson Library for Stella Gentry Sharpe turned up a 1947 *Tobe* story published in a periodical, *Pictures and Stories*, by The Methodist Publishing House and another easy reader, *Tildy*, published in 1965. Neither of these had the charm of the original *Tobe*, lacking the photographs by Charles

Farrell. In my opinion, Farrell's photographs elevated *Tobe* from other children's books of the period, which I am sure entranced children enough for them to stay with the pictures long enough to listen to and ponder over the text. In that respect, I think that perhaps *Tobe* was enjoyed by many school children who may have remembered it fondly and in that respect, it may have paved the way for more books about African American families. Stories engage our social emotions, which in turn teach us how to react and behave when we are faced with adversity (Greene, 2013). Stories that reflect our lives and circumstances are vitally important, especially if the reader belongs to a minority, whether that minority is different ethnically, racially, in religious practice, gender expression or sexuality. So, do writers have to share the same ethnicity or orientation as their characters to fully express the thoughts, emotions, and physical sensations in written language? At the table, we asked ourselves, "Whose story is it? Who gets to tell it?"

### Text to World: Since the creators were white, is this a positive portrayal of African Americans? Was it seen as a positive portrayal then? Is it one now?

Was this well-intentioned book simply another example of cultural misappropriation? The real problem of misappropriation in terms of children's literature is that authors and illustrators of cultures not represented in the book might indeed harm a child by presenting a warped worldview. At our table one student was concerned that inadvertent power dynamics would be recreated when someone misappropriated material from another culture, something Augusta Baker (1971) wrote about in 1971:

> The depiction of a black person is exceptionally important in books for children. An artist can portray a black child—black skin, natural hair and flat features—and make him a stereotype and caricature. The black child who sees the picture which ridicules his face may be deeply hurt, feel defeated, or become resentful and rebellious. The white child who sees the stereotyped presentation of the black person begins to feel superior and to accept this distorted picture or type. (Miller, 2003, p. 9)

If we applied the same criteria for evaluating *Tobe* as we would to any other picture book, we would ask: (a) does this work show excellence in literary quality; (b) does the artwork demonstrate excellence of quality in terms of technique;

(c) does the artwork enhance the text of the book; and (d) do both the illustrations and the text show respect for as the American Library Association (ALA) puts it, a child's "understandings, abilities, and appreciations"? (ALA, 2014, May 23). In short, if we applied the same criteria to *Tobe* as we might to every other children's book, would those criteria be enough to help readers determine cultural authenticity? Does *Tobe* demonstrate literary quality? No. The text is composed of simple sentences with a limited vocabulary, clearly meant to be a basal reader. The voice seems to be authentic to a little country boy. The photographs in the hardback edition of the book are sharp and clear; they clearly illustrate the text. The photographs must have been done over a period of months in order to capture the seasons of farm work, probably from May through November, based on which crop was being harvested and were interesting for some members of my table, who enjoyed the depictions of country life. In that sense, the story is "universal," a sense of commonality between the races, of being human, neither black nor white. But whether it is due to the nature of the work (i.e., a basal reader modeling standard English) or the outsider perspectives of both the writer and the photographer, *Tobe* lacks cultural authenticity in the both structure of language and the posed quality of the photographs. But the writing and photos seem to be sensitive to and respectful of the culture being represented. In that respect, *Tobe* certainly was progressive for the time.

Our table pondered whether it would be considered progressive today. What story would Tobe's family tell if this story was told today? I wonder if the voice of the story would have proudly reclaimed the local Southern dialect and phrasing. I think I have to look at works like writer Eloise Greenfield in *Childtimes*, Sherley Anne Williams *Working Cotton*, or the family stories of storyteller Jackie Torrence, and seamstress Nellie "Chubbs" Miles. In comparison to the richness and detail of culture expressed by these women, *Tobe* does not compare well. I also think that more realism about poverty or race might have made it into the stories if we told it today. We asked ourselves at the table if this story had been told about a white family, would these images be considered positive, but could not bring ourselves to answer. The unpalatable truth is that the class divisions of southern society of the time would have placed white tenant farmers above black tenant farmers. So, would this be considered an ideal way of living? No, even during the time when the median family annual income would be about $1,000, tenant farmers and sharecroppers would have been one-third of that. But all that is from an adult perspective, cognizant of the social and economic differences between an educated white woman and a young black boy. If *Tobe* was able to show school children that African American families lived similar lives to white children, then I would consider it both a positive work and progressive for its era.

Judi Morellion (2003), in her essay "The Candle and the Mirror: One Author's Journey as an Outsider," talks about the controversy of being an outsider, writing about a culture not her own and uses the metaphor of candle and mirror to describe the difference between an outside author who brings to light a culture or community with her writing or a writer who uses writing to reflect her community outward, to share culture as a member of that community. Morellion realized that the best "candle" she could provide was accuracy in her use of the English language to describe the beliefs, worldview, and environment of the Tohono O'odham people in her multivoiced poem. She worked with a Native American publisher and in the end commissioned a Tohono O'odham artist to illustrate the poem. In short, she tried her best as an outsider to be accurate in her portrayal of a society and she used as many resources as she could find to build validity into her work. For all of that, Morellion still received hate mail from people who claimed that she had misrepresented Native Americans. Now, I do not know whether Sharpe had insider knowledge about the African American culture; I am not even sure cultural misappropriation was a consideration at the time of publication. In all fairness, I do not know whether any African Americans in the area would have had as many socio-economic resources as Sharpe did to bring a book like *Tobe* into print and to fund its distribution; after all we are talking about the South in the mid-1930s. According to John McLeod of the UNC Press, it was a top-seller in its time and probably made its way into many classrooms, libraries, and homes, and I imagine, delighted many children.

In my observations, exposure to alternative viewpoints through fiction and media make other people seem less strange and foreign; as people become more familiar with other cultures through fiction, art, music, media, and food, they can begin to find empathy and common ground for understanding one another. So, the inclusion of works by authors and illustrators of people of color is not just crucial to our own self-acceptance, but also in helping to create understanding with those of other races and beliefs. Realistically, the first wave of children's literature to feature minorities were created, published, and distributed by the dominant culture and re-enforced damaging stereotypes.

But, as one of my tablemates pointed out, the children who would have seen *Tobe* were of the same generation that as adults, would have participated in civil rights protests. Perhaps the work of Sharpe and others like her signaled the beginnings of change. We do need to increase the representation of authors and illustrators of color so that children will have more exposure to African American writers and artists. More important, books by black authors and illustrators will be a better mirror to reflect black lives, lives that are not the stereotypes frequently portrayed in popular and social media. But we have to recognize that sometimes outsiders do a good job representing subculture. We need to have great books in every library, every school, every classroom, and in every home by good writers and illustrators, regardless of ethnicity or race—so we are surrounded and inspired by books and images that can teach us to reach out to one another, find our inner strengths, and be catalysts for change.

## References

American Library Association. (2014, May 23). "Caldecott Medal—Terms and Criteria." Retrieved June 27, 2017, from
http://www.ala.org/alsc/awardsgrants/bookmedia/caldecottmedal/caldecottterms/caldecottterms.

Greene, Joshua. (2013). Moral Tribes: Emotion, Reason, and the Gap between Us and Them. New York: Penguin Press, 59.

Miller, Marilyn L. (2003). *Pioneers and Leaders in Library Services to Youth: A Biographical Dictionary.* Westport, CT: Libraries Unlimited.

Morellion, Judi. (2003). *The Candle and the Mirror: One Author's Journey as An Outsider.* In Fox, Dana L., and Short, Kathy G. (eds.), *Stories Matter: The Complexity of Cultural Authenticity in Children's Literature.* Urbana, IL: National Council of Teachers of English.

# Tobe

Perspectives and Themes

TISHA GREENE | OAKHURST STEAM ACADEMY

As a young child and avid reader, I often struggled to find books that depicted characters who looked and acted like me. I read such books as *Nancy Drew*, *The Little House on the Prairie* by Laura Ingalls Wilder, *Encyclopedia Brown*, and books by Walter Dean Meyers, yet there were few books with characters with whom I could relate as a young African American girl from North Carolina. When the opportunity arose to participate in a book club and discussion for *Tobe*, a book published in 1939 written by Stella Gentry Sharpe that depicted the life of an African American family from North Carolina, I realized how powerful and important this discussion and my participation would be to addressing the lack of books depicting minorities. Knowing this history, *Tobe* represents an important shift in the literary landscape for all readers.

As someone with a background in English and language arts, I also pondered during the discussion how *Tobe* could be best taught within the context of elementary, middle, and high school social studies and English classes, so that the book itself can live on and more people can be exposed to the text. During the book club discussion, many participants shed light on stories that were passed down from their families. What emerged from our discussion was how important telling one's story is to ensuring both an accurate portrayal and that the narrative continues to live on through future generations.

## Text to Self:
## Did Tobe Accurately Portray Rural African American Life?

At the beginning of the discussion, most participants shared the belief that *Tobe* was not an accurate portrayal of the life of an African American family who sharecropped for a living in 1939 rural North Carolina. "There is research to say that Latinos and African Americans talk about bad stuff and good stuff. This is very strawberry. There is a more juicy story," said Diana Leyva, a book club participant.

Other participants compared the language in *Tobe* to that of the language in the *Dick and Jane* series. These books were comprised of sentences with a subject and verb and very little descriptive words. Many book club participants felt like this type of sentence structure and lack of descriptive language was a departure from the way most African Americans spoke and told stories during this time period. Based on the discussion and my own knowledge, I also agreed that the story did not necessarily reflect the voice of Tobe as I envisioned. I along with other book club members wondered what might be different if Tobe himself was able to tell his own story?

Through our discussion, there were many themes and concerns that were raised by participants, but one theme that emerged through my observation of the discussion was the difference in reaction to the book based on the generational differences of the book club members. Those who had a closer generational link to the time period of *Tobe*, perceived the book in a much different way than those who read the book and did not have the same real-life context. Some participants were able to give glimpses of their own experiences of picking cotton or growing up in poverty both in rural and urban settings. One participant indicated that he believed the simplistic language found in *Tobe* was a result of the author trying to make the book appropriate for a young child's reading level. Others believed that the language was due to a white person writing their perspective of Tobe's life.

Several participants talked about the differences between rural and urban life and the activities depicted in the pictures that corresponded to the text. One participant talked about the difference between living in poverty in a rural town and living in poverty in the city. He discussed how even though he grew up in poverty, he still found joy. He would do back-flips off of mattresses with his friends and family. This countered the belief of some of the participants that the pictures were staged because they showed happiness even though the family was in poverty. We pondered if the pictures were taken to fit the text, or if the text was the driving force for the pictures? We discussed some of the background information we had about the book, including information that the original pictures taken by Gentry Sharpe were lost. We also discussed the impact of staging the pictures on the book, since it was known that the photog-

Eli Davis considers the content with his group.

rapher was not able to take pictures of the original family on which the book was written. We also discussed the images depicted in the pictures and the lack of voice made many participants agree that the book reflected Gentry Sharpe's interpretation of Tobe's perspective.

Discussing this background information about the book allowed participants to share their own personal connections to the time period and the activities of the family of Tobe. Through the discussion and the personal connections identified by the book club members, it was also clear that we all agreed that *Tobe* represented Gentry Sharpe's interpretation of the family and their daily life.

Those who understood what life was like for both African American and white families in the South in the late 1930s and 1940s indicated that the life painted for the main character Tobe and his family was idealistic compared to their actual experiences. Many expressed that there was pervasive racial conflict at this time. One participant said, "I was born in 1942 and it [the book] was very simplistic, there was no struggle." The participant went on to say that the life of Tobe did not accurately depict the struggle that existed among African American families trying to make a living to raise and feed their families.

Another participant said that he had a positive experience when reading the book because it reminded him of his childhood experiences of walking in the woods. The participant indicated that the events in *Tobe* reminded him of friends, family, and them doing things together. Yet other participants compared the simplistic language of *Tobe* to the simplistic language found in the *Dick and Jane* readers. These popular basal readers introduced new words one at a time to young readers and were known as primers. Because of the time period in which *Tobe* was written, many book club members believed that Gentry Sharpe fashioned the simplistic language of *Tobe* after similar language used in the *Dick and Jane* readers, as well as her knowledge and training as a school teacher, to ensure the book could be read by young students.

## Text to Text:
## Looking within the Text for Representative Voices and Images

The publication of *Tobe* is not without controversy. As referenced during our discussion, one of the difficulties many at my table encountered while first reading the book was the narrative. As a native North Carolinian and someone very familiar with the dialect of rural Piedmont North Carolina, the language seemed too simplistic and prose-like for a young African American boy. Sentences are short with minimal dialogue and there are very few compound or complex sentences. As reflected in our conversation, this simplistic language and lack of description is a detour from the everyday vernacular of most African American families. Most participants believed the dialect present in the book does not reflect that of a sharecropping family on a farm in the 1930s but rather Gentry Sharpe's interpretation. Some of the participants compared the language in *Tobe* to books they read as children with very "strawberry, vanilla, and plain" text. There was little description or opportunities for Tobe, or those with whom he interacted, to actually interject their voice, beliefs, or feelings.

After reading the book and conducting some research on the author, Gentry Sharpe, it became clear that her portrayal of the life of a sharecropping African American family was far different from the book club participant's belief of such a family in 1939. While the many activities of the family that were portrayed in the book seemed to be consistent with that of a sharecropping family (picking cotton, attending church, tending to farm animals, harvesting in fields, and playing around the farm) the omission of the voice of the characters in the book made it difficult to hear an authentic voice in the text.

Although Tobe is the main character and tells the story of life on the farm in the 1930s with his family, most participants agreed his voice was actually that of Gentry Sharpe. As the title character, Tobe tells the reader what happens in his daily life on and off the farm. Most of these activities are based on the work of his family and his interactions with them. There is also no mention or interaction with the farmowner, people in the town, or Tobe's understanding of the laws and practices between African American and white people during this time period.

Even the few negative reactions and interactions Tobe has on the farm are told in a positive frame. Specifically, Tobe mentions to his mother that he does not like to pick cotton on page 58, and that he is hungry in the field. There is little explanation or context provided as to why Tobe does not like to pick cotton and why this same displeasure is not felt when picking sweet potatoes, harvesting tobacco, or completing other chores around the farm. There is also no mention of the heat that one working in the tobacco fields or the cotton fields would encounter at that time of year. After Tobe indicates that his arms are getting tired from picking cotton, the text immediately shifts to them eating lunch and the fact that the cabbage and potatoes were good. When Tobe asks his mother why he has to pick cotton, she replies that his father plants cotton so that he can buy clothes for Tobe to wear to school. Once Tobe's curiosity is satisfied, he says he will pick the cotton.

While *Tobe* provides very little of a representative narrative of the title character, it also omits the authentic voice of Tobe's family members and friends. While the book is told from Tobe's point of view, most books add the additional voice of secondary characters to include the feelings and actions of such characters. We agreed in our book club group that doing so would have given the characters more life and made the events depicted in the book more believable. On pages 81–83 as Tobe interacts with his family during Christmas, there is little mention of happiness, joy, or excitement for the holiday or presents.

Participants also noted some things that provided pause within the book to question whether or not things were as rosy as they seemed from the text. One such thing was the picture of "Mother's Cow" on page 33. The cow looks extremely emaciated. Other participants mentioned the lack of shoes in most of the pictures of Tobe and his brothers as another sign that they were a family in poverty.

The more I read *Tobe* and reflected on the conversations during the book club meeting, the more I wondered if this was intentional on Gentry Sharpe's part. Could the lack of expression actually represent the fact that few African American families were actually happy about their circumstance at this time? Because there is little historical information known about the family nor is there much information available about Gentry Sharpe, it is hard to determine how she felt about the laws and practices at this time or if there was hidden meaning in the lack of expression.

After conducting some research and coming upon a discussion titled "Tobe: An African American Children's Book Ahead of Its Time," and listening to a leading researcher who interviewed members of the family depicted in the book as well as the family of those featured in the pictures, it was evident that *Tobe* was celebrated in the African American community when it was published. The family members of the people depicted in the pictures would celebrate the book and ask for it to be read to them often. One of the speakers indicated that she would ask her mother to read the book to her over and over again (Michaels and Stasio, 2014). This observation indicates that Gentry Sharpe may have been trying to address negative stereotypes of African Americans during the time period as well as attempt to provide the community with a positive story to counteract those stereotypes. The book became a beacon of hope among the Goshen community and other rural communities in North Carolina because it was the first to depict African Americans in a positive light.

## Text to World: Using *Tobe* within K–12 Classrooms

*Tobe*'s recent resurfacing provides teachers with an opportunity to introduce the text into classrooms across multiple grade levels. Because it has a simplistic storyline and language with relatively easy readability, it is a suitable book for students in grades two and beyond. Yet if one looks between the pages and really delves into the historical significance of the book and the time period, this text could be used in middle and high school language arts and social studies classrooms to teach a variety of subjects and spark student conversation, debate, and forms of argumentative writing. *Tobe* could also be used to help students tell their own story as a mentor text for narrative writing. This work could specifically be done at the lower grade levels and as a reminder of what happens when one doesn't tell his or her story at the upper grade levels.

Before *Tobe* can be explored in the classroom, it would be important for teachers to identify the background knowledge necessary to allow young readers to best access the text. To ensure that students have enough background knowledge on the time period, teachers should explore how the geography of North Carolina, and its laws, practices, and policies shaped the life of African American families in North Carolina. It would also be important to let students know that during this time, white and African American families were segregated by laws that led to unequal treatment of African Americans.

Teachers could introduce the book by providing students with relevant background knowledge about the time period in which *Tobe* was set as well as providing students with pictures of the rural landscape, agricultural maps of the Piedmont region of North Carolina, and historical information about segregation and social issues of the time period. Some ways to introduce the time period and the context might be to find relevant newspaper articles from the 1930s and early 1940s.

After providing some background knowledge on the text, teachers might approach the book by having students read the text and then determining what type of text the book represents. At first glance, *Tobe* appears to be a work of nonfiction told by the title character. Once students have more information about Gentry Sharpe and her relationships to Tobe and his family, students might determine that the book, rather than being a biography, is more a work of realistic fiction. This could be the first point of debate, point counterpoint, or argumentative writing that teachers assign students.

The book provides multiple themes that can be explored by students using multiple mediums such as discussions, debates, and essays. The book also provides opportunities for students to formulate strong opinions or positions, without regard to who is or is not correct. *Tobe* also provides teachers with opportunities to integrate multiple subjects with the book such as history, social science, and geography. Another way to approach teaching *Tobe* might be to ask students if the book represents a primary or secondary source and why? Students might find that some elements in the book are presented as primary sources, for example the photographs of Tobe and his family. Others might determine that in the current context, the book is a secondary source including the photographs.

Although *Tobe* presents readers with simplistic sentence structure and readability, there are many complex themes found within and that can be derived from the text. These topics might be most appropriate for students at the middle grades and above. As students interact with the text, they could formulate questions that can be later turned into themes. For example, whose voice is present in the book; or, as a reader, what does the book represent? As students

Wide shot of Billingsville Rosenwald School on a beautiful April afternoon.

Old meets new at the Billingsville Rosenwald School/Grier Heights Community Center.

continue to access the complex themes in the text, they could lead them to the creation of their own narrative or that of someone else's. This process could create an opportunity to evaluate the argument of what happens to our story when we allow someone else to tell it. Is it as accurate as it would be if we told our own story and why or why not?

## References

Michaels, Will, and Stasio, Frank. (Writers). (October 14, 2014). *Tobe: An African American Children's Book Ahead of Its Time,* on *The State of Things,* radio broadcast. Chapel Hill, North Carolina: WUNC.

CPSIA information can be obtained
at www.ICGtesting.com
Printed in the USA
LVHW041709150819
627784LV00003B/198/P